John Welch, O. Carm.

IMMERSED IN MYSTERY

Articles For An Interior Life

Carmelite Media

Layout and Cover design by William J. Harry, O. Carm.

© 2025 by Carmelite Media
Printed in the United States of America
All rights reserved

No part of this book may be reproduced, stored in a retrieval system, or transmitted in any form, or by any means, electronic, mechanical, photocopying, or otherwise, without the prior written permission of the publisher, except by a reviewer, who may quote brief passages in a review.

Carmelite Media
8501 Bailey Road
Darien, Illinois 60561

Phone: 1-630-971-0724
Email: publications@carmelnet.org
Website: carmelites.info/publications

Printed Edition ISBN: 978-1-936-742-35-6

Table of Contents

Preface iii

PART ONE
PATTERNS OF GRACE

1. Telling Our Story 3
2. The Pattern of Life 7
3. Failure, Is It Necessary? 9
4. Phases of Faith 11
5. Senior Spirituality 13
6. Stuck in the Past 15
7. Journeys of the Soul 17
8. The Elder Son 21
9. Willful to Willing 25
10. Vacation or Pilgrimage 27
11. Two Mysteries: God and Self 31
12. The Symbolic Life 33
13. Be Perfect? 37
14. Once Were Warriors 39
15. Everyone Has a Vocation 43
16. Life, Spent or Hoarded? 45
17. Amazing Grace 47
18. Principles of Immigration 49
19. Two Essentials in Life 53
20. Carry Your Burden, and Mine Too! 57

PART TWO
AN INTERIOR LIFE

21. A Simple Way to Pray 63
22. The Value of Silence 65
23. The Desert 69
24. A Healing Presence 71

25. The Seven Capital Sins 73
26. Earning God's Love 77
27. Make America Good 79
28. Three Feasts in October 81
29. Sacred Places 83
30. Christmas: A Feast of Presence and Love 85
31. Summing Up the Year of Mercy 87
32. The Practices of Lent 91
33. Time to De-Clutter? 93
34. Resurrection 95
35. Father Michael McGivney 99
36. St. Bonaventure 103
37. Elijah, the Prophet 107
38. Joseph, the Dreamer 111
39. A Minor Order: The Carmelites 115
40. Memories of the Seminary, Civil Rights, and
    a "Contemplative Prophet" 117

Afterword 121

PREFACE

The brief articles in this work were first published in *Christ Is Our Hope*, a magazine of the Catholic diocese of Joliet, IL. The magazine was published monthly and I had the privilege to write an article for almost each issue over a twelve year period. The goals of the magazine were to evangelize and to educate. The magazine went to 170,000 families each month.

With no intention of writing a book, and with a modest but flexible goal of 600 words, I had ample time each month to choose a topic, study it, write a draft, listen to it for flow and balance, and have it proofed. Consequently, I have a reasonable confidence that the articles are readable and informative. Seventy of the articles were published by Paulist Press in *An Interior Life* (2022). An additional forty of the articles are in this work, published by Carmelite Media, William J. Harry, O. Carm., editor. The articles "Elijah, the Prophet" and "Joseph, the Dreamer" have also been published in *Carmel Notes: A Compendium of Carmelite Spirituality* (Carmelite Media, 2022). These articles were slightly expanded to describe Carmel's special relationship to each of these biblical figures.

I have arranged the articles in two parts, *Patterns of Grace* and *An Interior Life*. Because I was free to choose a topic each month the articles were written randomly and are disparate. They defy grouping. But they are an attempt to explore themes and persons having to do with an interior, spiritual life.

Pope Francis, in an address to Carmelites gathered for a General Chapter in Rome, said "Carmel is synonymous with the inner life" and he encouraged Carmel to pay special attention to the spiritual journey of persons. Writing for *Christ is our Hope* was a wonderful opportunity for a Carmelite.

PART ONE

Patterns of Grace

1

TELLING OUR STORY

Occasionally, when we had guests in the house, my father would grab a guitar (which he could not play) and announce: "Now hear my song!" He strummed once, proving he could not play, and put the guitar down, satisfied he had gotten everyone's attention.

Something in us wants to "sing our song." We want the music of our lives to be heard. We want the story of our lives told, and appreciated by others. And, as we age, our story gains momentum; it develops more twists and turns, surprises and disappointments. But often, when we try to tell others the story of our lives, we're not satisfied with the telling. We just cannot get it right.

Immersed in Mystery

One writer, Jerry, spoke about the difficulty he had telling the good from the bad in his life. He hd a cancer diagnosis, which he judged to be a bad thing in his life. But, in the course of treatment and the adjustments he made in his life, so many unexpectedly good things happened to him. He looked back, and began to reassess his original judgment. Maybe what had happened to him was more positive than he thought. But, after many years successfully battling the cancer, he was diagnosed with another complication, and he needed a heart transplant. The news was unwelcome! The "good" had once again turned "bad."

Jerry came to this conclusion: it is very difficult to judge what is good, and what is bad in our life. We are immersed in mystery. We struggle to make meaning of the events in our lives, and we are frustrated when we cannot. We hate to lose control over our life. On the other hand, when we accept the fact that we cannot tell our story in all its depth, then a great freedom can come into our life. We realize we do not have to make an accurate assessment. We can live without trying to figure our lives out precisely. We go on, immersed in mystery.

The Song of Creation

Saint Teresa of Avila wrote: "Lord I cannot know you unless I know myself; but I cannot know myself unless I know you." We can try to "sing our song", but, ultimately, we are a song being sung by God. We only know who we are when in relationship with that Holy Mystery. In that relationship we gain an accurate perception of ourselves and the world.

Saint Thomas Aquinas believed that every part of God's creation has a story to tell, a song to sing. Animals, plants, rocks, all have been given a "mission" by God. We humans interact with the rest of God's creation forming a complex story. We know parts of that story, but we cannot step back and read the grand narrative God is writing. Our little ego-drama has to give way the great Theo-drama, the ultimate storying of our life.

Everything Belongs

It is a great freedom to be unable to sum-up our life. Often, we feel we have not accomplished what we should have in life. Or, our life is colored with regrets, opportunities missed, doors closed. Even a "successful" life has many holes in it, many parts we would not include in telling our story. The truth is, we are not good judges of our lives. We are terrible story-tellers when it comes to weighing the different parts and events of our lives.

One writer offered this faith perspective: at the end of our life everything belongs. When the final chapter of our life is written, there is nothing left out that should be included, and nothing in the story that should be left out. The former Archbishop of Canterbury, Rowan Williams, made this insightful observation: "A human life is given its unity and its intelligibility from outside: when God pulls taut the slack thread of desire, bonding it to himself, the muddled and painful litter of experience is gathered together and given direction." We do not have to make sense of our lives. It is up to God to sing our song, and we hope that music will be heard for all eternity.

A Story of God's Mercies

But, something in us wants to tell our story. My father had to sing his song. Maybe we are compelled to tell the story of our lives because they are the story of God. In rehearsing oft-told tales about our life, perhaps testing the patience of others, we are giving voice to God. Our telling is not simply to have a memoir, but it is to trace the finger of God in the twists and turns of life. If we see life as a gift from God, and governed by God's providence, then our story celebrates God, not our fumbling efforts. And, it does not have to be coherent.

When sitting down to write the story of her life, Saint Thérèse of Lisieux, the Little Flower, wrote, "I will sing of the mercies of the Lord." Our lives are not the story of our aches and pains, but the story of God's mercy. This merciful God accompanies us the whole way. Holy Mystery puts up with our failings, never walks away, forgives our sins, and makes sense of our lives. We have every reason to take up our guitar and announce, "Now hear my song!"

2

THE PATTERN OF LIFE

Our philosophy professor in the seminary defined life as "One darn thing after another!" On certain days that definition seems apt. But, is there more structure or flow to life than that? Is there any discernible pattern to our days on earth?

At times we experience life as a placid stream; at other times it is a whirlpool. Developmental psychologists speak of seasons and transitions. They say there are predictable patterns. As a person shifts from one phase of life to another, we may experience upheaval, confusion, a loss of direction. But then, life settles down again, for awhile.

As we mature, our poor ego has to weather and adapt to periodic storms. One prominent psychologist claimed there is no growth in consciousness without pain. Letting go of one life structure, as another season of life comes on line, is a painful process. Something is always lost when new life emerges.

Saints and Seasons

The Saints also noticed life's pattern of loss and growth. In their struggles they spoke of climbing a mountain, crossing a desert, or finding their way to a centerpoint. The saint speaks of life as a pilgrimage of faith, with recurring invitations to conversion. In conversion, the Christian is learning to turn his or her life over to God in trust.

The psychologist charts the psyche's growth into consciousness. The Christian understands this process as grace-enabled, allowing the Christian to hear God's invitation into life. The psychologist names flesh and blood issues encountered in human development. The Christian understands these issues, as painful as they may be, as occasions for opening our lives to God's merciful love.

Sometimes the saints boldly speak about "becoming God." Of course they always remain creatures, but their union with God is so intimate that they can no longer tell who is acting in their life, they or the Holy Spirit. Combining the psychologist and the saint, we could say the goal of human development is, ultimately, divinization, a growing participation in the knowing and loving of God.

The Paschal Mystery

A fundamental pattern of life Jesus offered us is his death and resurrection, which is referred to as the Paschal Mystery. Just getting through the day is often a cross. Staying true to one's humanity as it unfolds involves repeated letting go. But Jesus also promised the Resurrection, not avoiding the cross but through the cross.

In other words, the dying and rising of Christ, the Paschal Mystery, is inbuilt in human development. Being faithful to life as it comes to us, and faithful to our growth as human beings, involves death and resurrection. And in this process we are responding to God who calls us more deeply into our lives. Good Friday and Easter Sunday, cross and resurrection, become the rhythm of our days. For a Christian, the Paschal Mystery is the pattern of life.

3

FAILURE, IS IT NECESSARY?

Success is over-estimated, and failure is under-appreciated.

When I was a young boy I listened, with my father, to the Notre Dame football games. When they lost, which was infrequent in those days, I was distraught. So was my dad, but he would say "You don't win them all, Jack." And he added, "It's not good to win them all." Maybe so, but I still preferred an undefeated season.

We all want to succeed, no one wants to fail. Yet, we all have an intimation that failure, somehow, may not be all bad. As a matter of fact, failure may be a necessity. We do need successes and victories in life, but they may prepare us for the times we do fail and lose. Is there some truth in these folk adages? The only thoughts worth listening to are the thoughts of the ship-wrecked; You are only truly free when you have lost your reputation.

Individuals who have been battered by life may come to a point where they acknowledge their inability to make their lives go right, and they have to turn them over to Another. I remember my aunt, who spent years feeding her husband through a tube in his throat, saying "I don't know how anyone gets through life without faith!" Some of the most "real" and loving people I know have been brought to their knees in life, but now stand again in faith.

Failure may be inevitable if we wish to become mature and generous in life. It may be inevitable if we are going to be able to love God and our neighbor. Great joys and celebrations can strengthen faith, too. But, failure has a way of getting our attention, and it may be our path to true, trusting faith.

We struggle so hard in life to "make it" that we become very self-preoccupied, necessarily so. But, once we have constructed a life and all the parts are more or less in place, we may be self-satisfied and ego-centric. Loving God and neighbor means stepping outside our carefully constructed life. It means a "letting go", and no self-respecting ego is going to "let go" just because it is a good idea. We tend to continue to fortify our life and try to grow increasingly self-sufficient. Failure teaches us we cannot control life, we are not our own gods. If we want to go on, we have to step outside ourselves and acknowledge our need for a strength beyond us.

To love God means to live in a way which allows one's will to be shaped by God's will. It means allowing God to find us. God cannot find us if we are hiding in the "home" of our self-sufficient life. And the experience of loss or failure may be something we look back on with gratitude.

Failure, unbearable loss, humiliating defeat, deep disappointment may not aways be "setbacks" in life, but may actually move life forward in unexpected ways. These experiences may be as much a necessary part of life as inhaling and exhaling are to breath. The cross promised by Jesus to his followers comes in unexpected forms. Death and resurrection become the pattern of life as we share in the Paschal Mystery, the death and resurrection of Jesus.

To love God is not a matter of feelings. Nor is it a matter of beautiful thoughts about God. As in any love, there is only so much knowledge, so much data we can gather about the beloved. At a certain point, we have to simply surrender into the mystery of the other person. So it is with God. At a certain point in life, often after a life has started to show cracks, we have a golden opportunity to surrender to Mystery, with a truly biblical faith of trust and hope.

At that point, having gone through our personal hell and now lifted up by grace, we have something to say, not only in words but in the witness of our life. Love of neighbor now becomes truly compassionate. Instead of saying, That poor guy, or, Those poor people, we now can say, We poor! And we then wait in hope with all who wait in hope for God's mercy.

As Christians our boast is not in a trophy, or an Emmy, or an Oscar, or an Olympic medal. Our boast is in the cross of Christ through which we have true and ultimate victory. It carries with it the promise of a future when every season is undefeated, and every tear is wiped away.

4
PHASES OF FAITH

From Wonder to Holy Mystery

Faith is our total, trusting response to God's love. Or, as one writer put it, faith is the "acceptance, finally, of having been accepted all along." How we receive and express that love and affirmation depends upon our stage in life. Attempts have been made to identify general stages in faith development. The studies of James Fowler and Gabriel Moran have provided a framework

Children have a mythical approach to religion. For an infant, mother and father are among the first faces of God. Through these faces the infant learns he or she is loved and wanted, and the world is a safe place. The first few years of life are a time of wonder. The world shimmers with mystery. Fairy tales, stories of religious traditions, and religious celebrations help the child make sense of the world. This approach to faith has been called a "first naiveté."

Acquiring a Religion

In the school years imagination becomes less important and is replaced by more linear thinking. The young person learns the stories of his or her faith tradition. Who are our heroes and heroines? What are our rules? It is time to learn about, and practice, being Catholic.

The young person is part of many stories: the family, the faith tradition, the school, and the peer group, among others. In adolescence, with the arrival of abstract thought, the individual struggles to find a "story of her stories." This synthesis may result in the many stories being subordinated to one story. Or, the person may compartmentalize stories, and take on the values of whatever group she is with at the moment.

Another phase of faith begins, at the earliest, in late adolescence, and often does not emerge until a person is in his mid 30's or 40's, if ever. In this phase the believer is able to step outside the various stories in which he is embedded, and is able to critically reflect on the stories, taking personal responsibility for values, beliefs, and lifestyle.

Adult questions arise and challenge a childhood faith. It may be a time of "disbelief" as the young person looks for more satisfying answers. Sometimes a particular philosophy is more compelling. A temptation at this time is to find a group with a strong ideology whose dogmatic approach may absolve the individual from personal reflection and decisions.

Adult Faith

The philosopher Soren Kierkegaard observed that we assume as we grow older we will continue to understand more and more. But in our mature adulthood a critical moment is reached when it seems everything is reversed. We now understand more and more "that there is something which cannot be understood." Christian mystics report an experience of "knowing by unknowing."

The adult middle years and beyond open up challenges to faith. Life is experienced as complex and ambiguous, even contradictory. The person of faith learns to stand within the tensions. Prayer is a pondering, as was the Virgin Mary's prayer when visited by the angel.

The mature adult has the opportunity to approach the faith with a "second naiveté," letting the images, stories, and celebrations express for us realities for which we have no better language. The adult can re-appropriate the faith, hearing it at a deeper level.

Faith cannot simply be reduced to certainties and rational understanding. Ultimately, faith expresses a relationship with Jesus Christ. It is not about knowing much, but loving much. Eventually faith calls for surrendering into the Holy Mystery of God.

As this more contemplative faith emerges, it is accompanied by a wider freedom and a greater detachment. Gabriel Moran wrote, "Whether one's work is to design a cathedral, mop floors, govern a nation, or lie flat on one's back in pain, the human vocation is to stay at one's post and do the best one can. And after doing the best possible, the detached person takes no credit but returns glory to the source of all gifts." *(Religious Education Development)*

5

SENIOR SPIRITUALITY

Practices When Growing Older

Frank Cunningham has written Vesper Time, a personal account of wisdom born in growing older. Cunningham had been editor and publisher of Ave Maria Press, Notre Dame, Ind. His title, Vesper Time, is a reference to the evening prayer of the church, a lovely prayer when lamps are lit as darkness descends. In evening prayer, we review our efforts during the day, and discover God's blessings in it all. It is not yet Compline, the final prayer of the night.

The following brief lines are an attempt to distill some of the wisdom contained in Cunningham's book.

"Aging is about living into our memories, about seeking their meaning, about accepting and being kind to them," Cunningham writes. One of the tasks for memory is to learn to forgive and let go. He tells the story of Fr. Martin Jenco , a priest from Joliet, who had been working with Catholic Relief Services in Lebanon. Fr Jenco was mistakenly identified by Shiite radicals and held captive for 19 months. Cunningham, in his role with Ave Maria Press, had helped Fr. Jenco tell his story in his book, *Bound To Forgive*. Fr. Jenco writes that it is almost impossible to forget, but he was able to forgive.

Walking the Camino

Because the creation is suffused with God's presence, our relationships and our experience of the world are windows opening on God's grace. Cunningham's appreciation for the natural world deepened when he joined a group of friends, then all in their mid-sixties, to walk the 500-mile Camino de Santiago. The Camino is an ancient pilgrimage route in Spain associated by tradition with the Apostle St. James. Each day on the pilgrimage, Cunningham tried to "walk well" for a loved one, a friend, or someone who shaped his life.

Calling the Camino a "seminal event," Cunningham maintains a discipline of lengthy walks. For years, he has walked three to five miles almost daily. "Walking," he says, "is linear contemplation."

Well into his seventies now, Cunningham realizes he hasn't experienced the level of suffering and tragedy that others have endured. He wonders about his courage when faced with his own debilitating suffering. He quotes Chesterton who described courage as "a strong desire to live taking the form of readiness to die." Cunningham recounts stories of people who were inspiring in their acceptance of suffering. "All made the courageous choice to grow rather than wallow."

Diminishment

Growing older brings an experience of diminishing physical capacities, and, at times, the experience of being invisible to others. All of the diminishing and disappearing may offer the opportunity to explore our interior life. Cunningham reminds us of an observation by the Trappist monk, Thomas Merton: God waits for us in the silence, until all the noise quiets down.

As he ages, Cunningham finds he identifies with Graham Greene who said, in aging he had less and less belief, but more and more faith. Cunningham writes, "Certitude troubles me while mystery enchants." He has read enough books (it was his occupation) to know that proof for God's existence is elusive. "We don't deduce God's existence," he writes; "rather we intuit God's presence." For him, "God is an impenetrable Silence, an indescribable Absence, an elusive Absolute."

Cunningham concludes we need to accept our story. He writes, "Exploring deep truths involves reflecting on how experiences of love, compassion, hope, joy and truth have shaped our story." And he suggests, "What if we were to take on one of these truths and sit with it in the early morning light with a cup of coffee?"

6
STUCK IN THE PAST

It is very hard to let go of our past. Many of us live in the past, clinging to hurts, disappointments, and especially our guilt. The Lord is always calling us forward into our future, but we are stuck in our past. When we wallow in our past, we lose perspective. We miss the daily invitations to walk forward in faith. It is like trying to drive while always looking in the rear-view mirror.

The heart can make anything into an idol, into a false god. We can readily admit to making idols out of obvious things such as wealth and power, but to see the past as an idol may be more difficult. In our preoccupation with the past, in our obsessive rehearsal of it, the past becomes a "god." I worship at its altar and become enslaved by it.

When we cling to our past, we are actually exalting ourselves. We are making our lives, our sins, our wrong-turns so monumental we are sure the world has never seen such a mess, and that even God has walked away. Our ego can be inflated in telling our story in this grandiose way. Ego is good at making everything about "us."

Letting Go

We cannot change the past. And we are who we are because of it. We may even have to make amends because of it. But, what can change is our relationship to it. The past does not have to define us and hold us back. Letting go of the past can be a matter of simply being more aware of our attachment to it, and slowly, with the aid of grace, learning to live in the present.

Or, our fixation on the past may be such that only a crisis opens us to change, and a new perspective. A dark time may be the occasion for healing and a growth in wholeness. That surrender may come only after we realize we are powerless to extract ourselves from our past. In the confusion, then, our ego may be open to

God's love luring us past where we have found ourselves stuck. Some wounds of the past may require professional help, but that too can be a grace-enabled effort.

Our faith tells us the Paschal Mystery, the dying and rising of Christ, will be the rhythm of our days. Letting go of an unhealthy regard for our past can be one of those deaths that leads to new life. The very struggle we have with our past, and the discovery of God's mercy in that struggle, can help us be bearers of forgiveness and compassion for others. The truth of our lives is that we are loved by God in spite of everything. Mercy, forgiveness, and healing are always available.

The Bigger Picture

We do not have to make sense of it all. We are unable to connect the dots in our past. We cannot because we live immersed in Mystery. Only from the outside can our lives be made intelligible. God can take the jumbled pieces of our story, our ego-drama, and put them into their place in the great theo-drama, the story the Spirit is telling. Our lives are really the story of God's mercies.

Consider Israel's past. Israel continually rehearsed all the ways it had not been faithful to God. But, the important memory was about all the ways God had been faithful to Israel.

> The prophet Isaiah said:
> Thus says the Lord:
> Remember not the events of the past;
> the things of long ago, consider not.
> See, I am doing something new.
> …It is I, I, who wipe out,
> for my own sake, your offenses;
> your sins I remember no more.
>
> (Is 43:18, 19, 25)

If God forgives and forgets our sinful past, what excuse do we have to remember it? Of course we will not have amnesia. But, what we will remember from the past are the blessings, the miracles that accompanied our days and years. We will remember when we were brought from slavery into freedom. And this memory will allow us to live the present in peace, and to anticipate the future without fear.

7

JOURNEYS OF THE SOUL

Our relationship with God is dynamic. It is variously described as, growth in holiness, spiritual development, living a Gospel life, putting on Christ. This evolving relationship with God is often expressed as a journey. Our Christian tradition has various ways of imaging the journey. Here are a few of the images:

Across a Desert

The starkness of a desert captures times in life when we may be in transition.

Our normal resources and strengths are failing us. The landscape of our life seems barren. But, the starkness of desert allows for clarity. Silence and solitude can be conditions for listening to our life, and to God, more deeply. The usual distractions are eliminated. Insights and possibilities may shimmer in the distance. This journey requires patient endurance. The desert, tended, may become a garden. The Jewish people moved from slavery to freedom through a desert.

Up a Mountain

In this image, God is living on the heights. We are beginning in the foothills. The ascent to God appears challenging and perhaps arduous. The safety of the ground and known features of life are left behind. What seemed non-negotiable in life begins to fade in importance. We now have a different perspective.

Trappist monk, Thomas Merton, imaged his conversion and vocation as an ascent up a 'seven storey mountain.' He was referring to the Mountain of Purgatory in Dante's *Divine Comedy*. It is an inner mountain climbed by penitents. Merton wrote, "…There is only one vocation. Whether you teach or live in the cloister or nurse the sick, whether you are in religion or out of it, married or single, no matter who you are or what you are, you are called to the summit of perfection; you are called to a deep interior life…" *(The Seven Storey Mountain).*

Through a Dark Night

Sometimes called the 'apophatic way', or the way of unknowing. This image captures the hiddenness of God, and the lack of clarity in our journey of faith. We are unable to find our way by ourselves.

Although apparently referring to a difficult time in life, the dark night metaphor in the Christian tradition actually expresses a positive experience of God whose love is obscure to us. "The brighter the light, the more the owl is blinded," wrote Saint John of the Cross. Losing all visible signposts along the way, the pilgrim learns to journey with absolute trust in a night that becomes a better guide than day.

Along a Little Way

A path called 'a little way' is associated with the Little Flower, St. Thérèse of Lisieux. It can mean doing small things with great love; but it can also mean doing whatever we do, whether big or small, with absolute trust in a merciful God. It is a way of humility and simplicity.

Thérèse was convinced that God was not looking for people to punish, but for people who will open their lives to God's transforming love. To her sister Marie, who complained she did not have the deep desires Thérèse had, the Saint responded, "…The weaker one is, without desires or virtues, the more suited one is for the workings of this consuming and transforming love. …It is confidence and nothing but confidence that must lead us to love." *(Letters)*

Toward an Awakening

Perhaps a particularly apt image for our spiritual journey is an 'awakening.'

God is not distant; God has gone nowhere. God is a transcendent

Presence always in our lives. It is a matter of not hiding in our lives, but being available to God, allowing God to find us.

Jesus met the Samaritan woman at the well without preconditions. He accepted her, and her past. She testified, "He told me everything I have done" (Jn 4: 39). Similarly, the Lord meets us and accepts us where we are in our lives. In that realization we begin to 'awaken' to a mercy and love that has always been present.

A Basic Pattern

The Paschal Mystery refers to the salvific Life-Death-Resurrection of the Lord. In all of our journeys that sequence of life giving way to a dying which leads to renewed life is the recurring pattern. It is through our inevitable crosses, lived in faith, that we enter into the experience of resurrection. With God's help we learn to let go and live in trust. Pope Francis reminds us: "Life grows by being given away... ." *(The Joy of the Gospel)*

8

THE ELDER SON

> "He became angry, and ... refused to enter the house"
> *(Lk 15, 28)*

Henri Nouwen was a Dutch priest-psychologist whose writings in the decades following Vatican II provided spiritual direction for countless individuals. He taught at Notre Dame, Yale, and Harvard, lectured widely, and wrote numerous books. One of Nouwen's most popular books is *The Return of the Prodigal Son*, an extended reflection on Jesus' parable of a wayward son and a compassionate father (Lk 15, 11-32).

Nouwen had been drawn to Rembrandt's painting of this Gospel parable. His interest was such that he traveled to St. Petersburg, Russia, to study the painting now on display in the Hermitage Museum. Nouwen's book presents his reflections on the painting, and the biblical story. He describes the three main characters: the prodigal son who left for a 'distant country,' his compassionate father, and the elder son who stayed home. Nouwen identifies with each of them, and invites the reader to similar reflections.

The Elder Son

The younger son's destructive behavior is obvious. The father's compassionate love is manifest. It is the elder son, in particular, whose character calls for a more nuanced understanding of his mind and heart. The elder son is presented off to the side in the parable, as well as in Rembrandt's painting, a figure standing on the right, robed in red. His jealousy and anger will not allow him to enjoy his brother's homecoming. He will not enter the father's house to join in the celebration where there is music and dancing.

Nouwen describes the elder son as the son who stayed home, wanting to please by being dutiful. And now he carries resentment toward the younger brother who followed his own desires, neglecting the needs of the family. In his complaining, the elder son experiences his dutifulness as a burden, and his faithful service as servitude. He too is in a 'distant country,' though still on the farm. He is 'lost' at home. "And it is this lostness," writes Nouwen, "characterized by judgment and condemnation, anger and resentment, bitterness and jealousy – that is so pernicious and so damaging to the human heart."

The Return of the Elder Son

Nouwen identifies with this elder son, as may his readers to varying degrees. Healing and wholeness for elder sons (daughters) cannot come from themselves. The resentments are too deep to be rooted out. "[They] can only be healed from above," Nouwen says, "from where God reaches down."

Just as the father ran down the road to meet the son, the father goes out of the house to meet the elder son, and invites him into the celebration. He counters the elder son's sense of alienation, saying, "You are with me always." He does not love the younger son more than the elder son. "All I have is yours," he says to his eldest.

The father's love for his sons does not depend on their repentance or pleadings. The father only wants each to come home. "Home" is God's unqualified, unconditional love.

What brings us back from a "distant country"? Nouwen recommends trust and gratitude. We have to trust that God wants us to come home, to open ourselves to God's compassionate love. To trust requires discipline. We have to choose to go past our complaining and resentment; we need to decide that we are not neglected and unappreciated. We have to step into a trusting relationship with the One who is coming down the road to meet us.

Gratitude, too, requires discipline. Our resentment comes from our belief that we haven't received all that we have deserved. Gratitude tells us we have received an abundance of blessings. We can moan about our perceived slights, or we can celebrate our unearned, freely given gifts from God. It is our choice.

Nouwen's suggestion is to acknowledge small gifts that come to the fore, look for others, and step by step come to the realization that we are living a very blessed life, given us by a compassionate God. We are already "home"; now we need to live in it, and join in the music and dancing.

9

WILLFUL TO WILLING

A Journey of Conversion

Spiritual writers often describe the conversion process as a movement from willfulness to willingness. Willfulness can be the determined behavior of one who is self-centered and overly controlling. Willingness describes an attitude of one who is available to God, who surrenders in faith to God's will. The willful person is often trying to win God; the willing person allows God to find him or her.

We are encouraged to live life with a relaxed grasp. We have to use our willpower and make decisions; otherwise, we are at the mercy of events. On the other hand, too tight a grasp and we leave no room for the guidance of grace, God's loving presence. Any effort to totally control life is bound to fail. Perhaps we only learn to relax our grasp in failure. Grace does not rob us of our freedom or our responsibility to use our will. But it can lead us into a spaciousness where we are undefended and at the disposal of God's mercy.

A Christmas Conversion

A story in the life of St. Thérèse of Lisieux illustrates the difference between willful and willing. Therese experienced a conversion when she was thirteen years old. She was very young when her mother died. She had become overly self-involved, extremely sensitive, and was given to scrupulosity. She tried hard to please people. She cried easily, and then "I'd begin to cry again for having cried."

It was Christmas and the family had just returned from midnight Mass. Thérèse was preparing to engage in a family ritual of finding gifts in her shoes by the fireplace. But the father was annoyed, thinking Thérèse was too old for this game. As Thérèse was going upstairs to take off her coat and hat she heard her father say, "Well fortunately this will be the last year!" The words pierced her heart. Thérèse's sister, Celine, thought that Thérèse would break into a flood of tears. But, at that moment, unexpectedly, she simply did not cry. She was hurt, but she had the freedom to take a stand against her emotions. She entered into the Christmas ritual with enthusiasm, excitedly found the gifts in her shoes, and gave great delight to her father.

Thérèse had a strong will, to the point of being quite stubborn. She had tried to use this will to pull herself out of her sensitivities, but to no avail. She identified with the Apostles, "Master, I fished all night, and caught nothing." She realized it was sheer grace that allowed her to break the pattern. Her explanation: "Jesus took the net Himself, cast it, and drew it in filled with fish." In a moment, grace had taken her out of the small circle in which she had been perpetually tursing. She wrote that from the time of her Christmas conversion she was able to forget herself and be concerned for others. "He made me a fisher of souls."

The interaction between grace and our freedom is complex. The challenge to live with a willing heart is the challenge to be available to God. Being overly willful robs us of our freedom. We have an attachment to a pre-determined outcome. In our fixation, we may miss the grace offered us. Individuals caught in addictions tell us change begins in an admission of failure to control our behavior. This relaxing of our grasp gives grace an opportunity to work in us. St. Paul testified to the difference between willful and willing when he wrote, "So it depends not upon a person's will or exertion, but upon God, who shows mercy" (Rom 9, 16).

10

VACATION OR PILGRIMAGE?

I am convinced that many vacations are actually pilgrimages. We return to certain places time and again because they are restorative in ways other places are not. We are different when we are there, and when we return we know we have been in touch with other dimensions of our life. We know there is "more" to us, and "more" to our lives.

Pilgrimages have a similar effect. We journey to sacred places on this earth. The journey is away from home and the familiar, and toward a numinous place of expectation. Pilgrimage dislocates us, and allows us to decompress. We leave our normal routines and identities and place ourselves in situations not in our control. Cares may come with us, and may be the reason for the pilgrimage, but they are held differently, in hope. Pilgrimages are potentially powerful religious practices which allow us to express our faith, and to find faith renewed.

Journey to a Center

Pilgrimage is an ancient, universal human activity. The oldest site of human construction, recently identified, appears to have been a shrine, not a place of residence. Humans did not live there; they intentionally traveled to it. Humanity has continually grappled with the mystery at the core of its existence. The sacred defies capture.

Shrines generally have a predominant symbol, such as a particular image of Mary, mother of God. The dominant symbol gives flow to the journey and organizes the different experiences. Often, there are sub-symbols, way stations or chapels encountered on the journey to the shrine. Stages of the journey heighten the anticipation. Often, the pilgrim does not approach a shrine directly, but must circle it before entering the sacred space.

Inner Footwork

Whether it is to Assisi, Lourdes, or Einsiedeln, pilgrims journey toward a sacred center. The journey is toward a point where the divine and the human intersect in palpable ways. Christian pilgrimages replicate the way of the cross.

Pilgrimage is prayer of the feet. It is accompanied by inner footwork. Traveling to a sacred place on the earth evokes a parallel inner journey to the center of the pilgrim. The actual distance traveled may not be great. Anthropologists Victor and Edith Turner wrote: "…pilgrimage may be thought of as extroverted mysticism, just as mysticism is introverted pilgrimage" (Image and Pilgrimage in Christian Culture). The pilgrimage is marked by geography and history; the inner journey is marked by a growing attentiveness to Holy Mystery who calls our name.

A Language for Soul

Shrines constellate stories, rituals, imagery, and music. The senses are captivated, the emotions are given expression, the mind relaxes into a total experience. Dormant faith awakens as the soul finds a language for its deepest yearnings. And often, at their core, shrines evoke a sacred silence, the most expressive language of all.

Frequently pilgrimages are to places sacred in the experience of multitudes of people. The presence and faith of others contributes to the power of the place. Our Lady of Guadalupe draws enormous crowds whose various rituals and ways of honoring the Lady weave a rich, colorful tapestry of faith. A pilgrim may arrive numb, and leave vibrant.

Personal "Shrines"

However, a pilgrimage can also be quite personal. The destination of a personal pilgrimage may be considered a "shrine" only by the pilgrim. It may be a place of special experience, or significant memories. It may hold profound meaning. It is sacred to the pilgrim who is brought back in time and feeling when in that place, or who is put in touch with levels of life otherwise unknown. And it may evoke reverence, gratitude, or simply, stillness.

So, it is possible that many vacation destinations are actually shrines sacred only to the pilgrim/vacationer; they shimmer with renewal and mystery. And how impressed the neighbor is when we say, "I am going on pilgrimage!" We just don't tell them where.

In most places on the earth, the world is opaque and does not easily reveal its maker. In other place, the world is practically translucent and the divine shimmers through. Such are the "thin places" of the Irish. It often depends upon the willingness of the pilgrim to truly "see." Pilgrimage to a place sacred in experience and memory opens the world to its graced depths.

11

TWO MYSTERIES: GOD AND SELF

We live with two mysteries, God and ourselves. We fully comprehend neither, and spend a lifetime learning about each. St. Teresa of Avila said we cannot know God unless we know ourselves, but we cannot know ourselves unless we know God. We have to engage one mystery to know the other.

God is met in God's world. Let creatures speak to you of their maker, said Teresa. So, we go to God through God's creation. Since we are the first part of God's creation we encounter, in coming to know ourselves we grow in our understanding of God. One theologian observed that we know what we say to God in prayer, but do we know what God says to us? His conclusion is that we ourselves are what God says to us. God speaks us and in coming to hear more clearly the word that we are, we come know more fully the God who speaks us.

But this world cannot tell us who we are. Rather than coming to know ourselves from within, from the Mystery at the core of our life, we give ourselves away to outside gods and ask them to give us our identity. We ask the world around us to validate us. We point to what we have piled-up in our lifetime: possessions, trophies, bank accounts, titles, achievements. All good, but none of it God.

Who we truly are is known only in God. Our identity requires a life-long exploration into that Holy Mystery. Prayer is the context for finding our identity and worth. We need to go quiet and listen. At times, only when our support has been taken away are we available to God. When external and internal voices go quiet, we may hear the gentle whistle of the Shepherd.

God Delights in Us

The saints testified to a great change in their lives when they moved from the small island of their obsessive control into the surrounding ocean of God's mercies. When a relationship with God is nurtured in prayer, the world is seen more clearly. And we ourselves come into focus. You are worth more than many sparrows" (Mt 10: 31). Instead of having to prove our worth, we find we already have immense worth and dignity. God has judged us, along with all creation, as good. We need no other validation. Surprising things are learned. Instead of having to name ourselves, we find ourselves already named. With our brother Jesus, we are the Beloved of God. We are born precious in God's eyes. God delights in us.

Of course, we first know of God's love for us through the love of others. As God's messengers we have to tell one another how good we are and how much we are loved. We come to trust in ourselves when we experience the love of others for us. One writer describes this process of affirmation as "blessing" others. We bless others when we pay attention to them and, by word or deed, tell them of their goodness.

Ultimately, a relationship with God in prayer becomes the source of our deepening identity. The more we can say "God" in our life, the more we can say our own name with confidence and trust. The challenge to our faith is to accept that we are unconditionally loved by God. Surrendering in faith surprisingly leads to greater freedom and self-possession. We then bring that conviction and confidence to a world seeking its own identity and direction.

12

THE SYMBOLIC LIFE

> We meet ourselves in a thousand different disguises on the road of life.
>
> Carl Jung

The depth psychologist, Carl Jung, believed we have to find ourselves outside before we find ourselves inside. In other words, our interior life is first met outside of ourselves in someone or something. These objects or persons fascinate us, not simply because of their own qualities, but because they express something in us we have yet to acknowledge. In the words of the psychologist, they are "symbolic."

A symbol is a bridge to an unseen shore. We see this side of the bridge, whatever or whomever captivates us, but we don't see the other side of the bridge. The other side of the bridge is something in us which is finding expression in the symbol. Thinking we are engaging another we are actually coming to know ourselves. In meeting the other, we are actually meeting ourselves.

Falling in love is a privileged example of this dynamic. We are attracted to someone we may not know very well. We think we are being objective in our assessment, our falling in love. But, initially, the powerful attraction of the other derives from an unconscious relationship with ourselves. The numinous presence of the other person derives from the fact that in them we are coming home to ourselves, an enormously attractive journey. In time, the other person no longer carries for us what we have not owned in ourselves. We are able to love the other for their own qualities, not as symbols of our unmet inner life.

Sacred Figures

Jung, the psychologist, observed that the human psyche is ready for someone or something to be its "god." This readiness for a "god" means we have a need for someone or something to be central in our life, around which the rest of our personality is organized. The psychologist cannot say where this readiness originates. All he can say is if there is a god-imprint in the psyche, it makes sense there is an imprinter. Our Christian way of stating this reality was articulated by St. Augustine: "Our hearts are restless until they rest in Thee!"

Freud believed that when we outgrow our parents, we search for a "god" who is actually a Big Parent. In contrast, Jung believed that the god-readiness came first, and the first images which filled-in that readiness were the parents who became "little gods." The journey through life, according to Jung, is to find more and more adequate images for the god-readiness (or god-archetype) within us. Whatever figure or image that expresses for us the inner readiness for God takes on a powerfully attractive, numinous quality.

Sacred figures, such as a pope, have their own attractive qualities based on their personal attributes. But the numinosity of the papacy derives not only from the qualities of a particular pope, or the importance of the role, but also from our own hunger for the transcendent, for someone who speaks to us and holds for us our deepest desires.

Pope Francis

Pope Francis has captured the imagination and admiration of countless numbers of people throughout the world. The Papacy, in itself, commands attention, but the personal qualities of Pope Francis make him a particularly appealing leader of the church. His simplicity and courage, and his appeal to watch out for the vulnerable and neglected of the world resonates with the goodwill of people.

In this admiration for the Pope we learn about ourselves as well. We realize the depth of our hunger for meaning and goodness in life. We resonate with the Pope's affirmation of the goodness of God's creation and the immense dignity of every human being. Pope Francis speaks to our best selves and encourages us to witness in our lives what is most deeply held in our hearts.

13

BE PERFECT?

One reform of a religious Order had as a motto, More unity, less perfection! The men of the reform were enthusiastic and deeply sincere about their Christian living. But when enthusiasm is translated into striving to be "perfect", then the spiritual life can become a competition. It is simply another ego-driven contest which may lead to comparisons and judgments, and unity suffers. Such a high bar may also lead to a sense of being unworthy.

"Be perfect," said Jesus, "just as your heavenly father is perfect." He said these words at the conclusion of an exhortation to love enemies. It is not about being morally superior to others; it is about recognizing our shared poverty and dependence upon God, and loving others with compassion.

When the spiritual life is portrayed as a rugged, ascetical, ascent to heroic virtue it becomes too daunting. So many people have said, "I would like to live a spiritual life, but right now my life is a little mixed-up. When I get back on track, then I will be able to be more spiritual." The acknowledgement of being "unready" is already the beginning of the journey.

When presented with stories of Saints who attained great achievements, we may admire them, but probably are not inclined to imitate them. We feel defeated before we start. Live with lepers on a peninsula in the middle of the ocean? Not likely! I have trouble living with people who are in the next room!

When a saint is beatified or canonized, what is being recognized? Is it achievement, or is it desire? Probably both. But I know the story of a foundress of a religious congregation who had little to show at the end of her life. She wanted to serve the Lord, but had trouble finding the right situation. She recruited young women in the hopes of founding a teaching community. She worked to establish a school to provide needed education for young children. It was a time of opposition to the church in her country. Politics intervened. Her fledgling community was suppressed and her sisters sent to their homes. At the end of her life, this woman left a trail of unrealized dreams, and her community consisted of two other women sharing her dream. Yet, she was beatified by the church.

On what basis was she beatified? It could not simply have been her achievements. True, her efforts eventually led to the establishment of a dynamic religious community. It was a testament to her spiritual qualities and her witness to the Gospel. But this community was only a dream when she died. What perdured during all the difficulties was her desire to be a conduit for the will of God. She wanted her will to be in sync with God's will, her desire to be one with God's desire for this world. It was a matter of faithfulness, not success.

Real Perfection

Yes, asceticism and discipline are important. We do have to work to make concrete in our lives the God-given desires we have. It is striving, it is effort, and it entails the cross. Time and again our ego gets bruised. In our graced efforts, we can make an opening in the world for God's love and compassion. With St. Ignatius of Loyola we can be "indifferent" to the outcome of our efforts. Meaning, we do care and we do energetically employ our gifts, but we have freedom regarding the results.

The real achievement in the spiritual life is surrendering to God's love. That love is freely given and can transform us. We have never needed to show a perfect life, or heroic achievements. It is simply trusting in God's all-conquering love. When we make our lives available to God, when we allow God to find us, then great things can happen. Such as unity and the perfection of charity!

14

ONCE WERE WARRIORS

Male Spirituality

Many women would wince at this statement: the world needs more masculine energy. If we see "the masculine" as responsible for aggression, bullying, and violence, then we might want less masculine rather than more.

But, some observers make a distinction between a boy-psychology and a man-psychology. The immature male as "boy" can be the one who is often self-destructive and detrimental to society. He may oscillate between abuse and weakness. The negative aspects of a patriarchal society, such as power, domination, manipulation, aggressiveness, and marginalization of women, manifest an immature masculine, a boy-psychology. However, the male as "man" inhabits a more mature masculine role. This masculine energy builds-up rather than destroys, protects rather than abuses, liberates rather than controls. This deeper masculine can be a blessing to both women and men.

Developmental psychologists point to the need for boys to be initiated into manhood. Father figures and rites of initiation have been the traditional means. In our times father figures are often absent, either physically or emotionally. And we no longer have transforming rites of initiation; we have mere ceremonies. The male may become an adult, but may also remain a boy.

Traditional stories, such as the story of the hero, speak to a boy's need to undergo tests in order to be an adult male. But defeating the enemy and winning the princess is not the end of male development. Some would say that the reason we never hear of the couple again is that the man does not know what to do with her. A further journey of transformation is needed to access a more mature masculine. It is the journey of the hero again, but into neglected regions of the masculine psyche. Other dragons need to be fought and other dark forests entered before a deeper masculine emerges.

The Warrior

Once Were Warriors is a film about the Maori in New Zealand. The Maori once were warriors; warrior was their identity and combat their duty. But the modern world does not need them to fight in the traditional way. Having lost their "myth", their self-understanding, the men have turned to weight-lifting, drinking, and abuse of others including their families. It is a disturbingly violent film. At the end of the film Beth leaves her abusive husband saying, "Our people once were warriors. But unlike you, Jake, they were people with manner, pride; people with spirit."

In the film, one of the sons is sent to a boys group home. A strong male director inspires the boys to look for inner strength and teaches them the Old Ways. Through traditional chants, myths, and martial arts he attempts to restore a transformed spirit and identity in the group. The warrior energy is acknowledged and re-appropriated to invigorate the community. You might look for a video showing Maori performing the Haka, a traditional war dance. For the participants it is cathartic, and a little unsettling for the observers. The New Zealand rugby team performs the Haka at its matches.

Myth, Ritual, Inner Work

In response to the needs in men today, one of the members in my community leads weekend workshops devoted to male spirituality. The men frequently participate in rituals, ceremonies using symbols, which help them experience places of "stuckness" in their development. They bring a new awareness to their lives. Father-hunger is acknowledged; losses are grieved, shadows are integrated. These processes allow the healing and enlivening power of God's Spirit to be acknowledged and called upon.

The psyche of the male has diverse energies which allowed him to fulfill the roles he was expected to play. Warrior is one, king is another, lover is another, so is priest. It is a spiritual process to access these energies through ritual and meditation and make them available in constructive, supportive, and loving ways. Myths and rituals, prayer and meditation, help us to re-tell our stories in ways that are healing and energizing. Men cannot defeat all the dragons, but they can battle many of the influences which today undermine families, coarsen society, and marginalize individuals and groups. The Kingdom of God needs its knights.

15

EVERYONE HAS A VOCATION

No matter what our path in life, the fundamental truth is we have been called into life. We have been summoned into a mystery which will take a lifetime to explore. We didn't simply fall into life. God freely loved us into existence. In a homily Pope Benedict said "each of us is the result of a thought of God. Each of us is willed, each of us is loved, each of us is necessary." We are of immense worth and dignity.

What we are called into is a relationship with God. We are called to holiness. Whatever path we take in life is a successful path if it allows us to awaken to that relationship. The relationship will transform us and propel us into service of our brothers and sisters and all of God's creation.

Life's Debris

The path to finally accepting God's love in my life may be cluttered with debris. My life may not appear successful in the eyes of others. It may be that certain dead-ends and even outright failures mark my path. The difficult times become the occasion for a serious reappraisal. The question may no longer be, what do I expect from life; the question becomes, what does life, and God, expect of me? How do I now respond to the circumstances of my life?

I may decide I have been on the wrong path for a long time. Making changes does not entail a laborious re-tracing of my steps. Gospel stories tell us Jesus meets us where we are, and offers us acceptance and love. Our challenge is to accept the love, and to allow that love to change us.

Some people hear a call and make radical breaks from their former lives. Albert Schweitzer, an accomplished scholar, lecturer, and musician, was challenged by the Gospel story of the rich man who lived in luxury, and Lazarus, the poor man who lived at his gate (Lk 16: 19-31). Schweitzer entered medical training, became a doctor, and opened a hospital in Africa, treating thousands of patients, including hundreds with leprosy.

Career or Vocation?

But is it possible to come to acknowledge our call in life without radically upsetting that life? For example, why can't there be a vocation within a career? We may serve a career by devoting all our energy to it, but is there a way of seeing that career as a service to a larger, transcendent reality? It is the rare job or path in life that does not in some way contribute to the lives of our brothers and sisters.

Rather than going abroad in our life to find our call, we might enter more deeply into the life we are already living. Perhaps we have half-listened to a call all along. Now we need to hear it more clearly and live it more intentionally. To outside eyes, nothing has changed. But looked at more closely, what has changed is how we are living our life. We are finding God, and God's will, in the dailyness of events. We have taken a path that has brought us back home.

Some individuals discern a call to directly assist others in their situations of need. Others, however, serve the world by developing a talent or a skill which in its own way brings life to others. Think of the baseball player whose skills delight followers of the game. Think of the architect, the landscaper, the business person, the homemaker. Lived as an expression of faith and in service of the larger community, these daily lives give glory to God. Ordinary tasks become acts of adoration and worship. And many people find ways to blend their day-job with more direct service of the poor.

Actually, the whole universe is summoned. Pope Francis reminds us that all creation has a vocation. "The entire material universe speaks of God's love, his boundless affection for us. Soil, water, mountains: everything is, as it were, a caress of God" *(Laudato Si, no 84)*. Our vocation becomes clearer when we see ourselves as part of a universe praising God by being itself.

16

LIFE: SPENT OR HOARDED

Life increases when we spend it; it decreases when we hoard it. Or, as Pope Francis in *The Joy of the Gospel* reminds us, "Life grows by being given away, and it weakens in isolation and comfort" *(Aparecida Document)*. The Gospel, too, reminds us, when we save our lives we lose them; when we lose our lives we find them. We have experienced the truth of this wisdom time and time again. It is true for any stage of life. But the maturing adult, particularly, is challenged to be generative, to give life away so that others may have life. Jesus reminded us there is no greater love.

The Young Person

We know the adage, you cannot give what you do not have. The first part of life has the task of accumulation: experiences, values, identity. Emerging from the womb of anonymity the very young person must acquire a sense of "I". Ego, at this stage, is a welcome and necessary development. This "I" has to learn to relate to other people and situate itself in the world. The young person has to try on roles or masks, a way of understanding oneself, and presenting oneself to the world. This persona is healthy when it is a combination of our best hopes, the legitimate expectations of others, and the very real possibilities of our personalities.

The Maturing Adult

It is the task of adult years to give life away. The difficulty will be to challenge a once healthy ego, which has now become ego-centric, to let go of its control. It begins to experience a law which demands that what has been accumulated now must be spent. This demand comes from within the personality as well as from outside. The demand from within comes from other levels of life now seeking expression. The demand from outside comes from the expectations and needs of other people. A carefully cultivated persona will have to give way to meet the new demands. Sometimes it is only when events dismantle the persona is the person open to new life.

One poor response is to identify so tightly with our persona, our self-understanding, that nothing and no one can break through. Perhaps when Pope Francis talks about discernment in life, and says we should not arbitrarily set the "edges" and pre-determine our journey's outcome, he is encouraging a loosening of control. We need to stay available for the Spirit's guidance. It is a delicate balance and has been described at times as, living life with a relaxed grasp, and, wearing the world like a loose garment.

The Cost of Generativity

When Jesus says his followers will have to take up their cross, he was not glorifying suffering. He was saying that to follow Him and love others will be costly. Care and concern for others, as well as our own maturation process, makes us vulnerable and pulls us beyond our own comfort. A psychologist once observed, "There is no growth in consciousness except through pain." This learning to let go inevitably means something is lost. And the letting go may be initiated by failure, loss, or deep disappointment. The greater part of our adult years will call for generativity, a spending of life so that life can flourish around us. Here is where talk of carrying the cross is appropriate.

Something feels "right" when life is shared. When we leave the shore of our security, unpredictable adventures are possible. Resurrected life is not just about the next world; it occurs whenever the desire to turn in on oneself is defeated and a person experiences freedom and strength to contribute to the well-being of the world. The dying and rising of Christ, the Paschal Mystery, is replicated in the struggle to give our lives away in unselfish service.

17

AMAZING GRACE

Grace is what makes us holy. Grace names a power or strength available to us, but from beyond us. Grace is often glimpsed only when our own strength is in doubt. At times, in the history of Christianity, grace was quantified and acted much like money in the bank. It could be gained, and it could be lost. Certain acts gained more grace than others.

The theology of grace has become more nuanced. No longer viewed as a quantity, or simply an effect in the soul, grace now is understood to refer to the presence of the Holy Spirit, along with Father and Son, in each person. Grace is God abiding in our depths.

Grace cannot be earned or achieved. It is the absolutely free, merciful, loving presence of God. It is pure gift, requiring nothing but gratitude. It is much like a sea which buoys all on the surface. This sea of grace gives our humanity a depth and a strength not always apparent on the surface of life. St. Augustine, known as the "Doctor of Grace", stressed the necessity of God's help in living a good life.

Grace, Always There

We often assume that in order to be a Christian we have to seek and find God. But the Saints, themselves products of grace, assure us that God is "always already there," seeking us. The challenge for us is not to find and win God, but to allow God to find us. We have to live in such a way that we are available to God.

This presence of God, grace, communicates merciful love. When we are self-sufficient and inattentive our need for this love is not apparent. But grace is there, sustaining us, supporting our efforts, even if rarely acknowledged. It comes to the fore, at times, when all else is gone, and strength is nowhere to be found. St. Paul, when faced with an intractable problem, heard the Lord say, "My grace is sufficient for you!" St. Paul's experience of being empowered by grace led to this conviction: "When I am weak, then I am strong" *(2 Cor 12)*!

We grow and deepen when we surrender to that power within our lives. When we stop living with the myth that we can totally control our lives and make them turn out as we wish, we then may be open to grace offered us. It is an antidote to feeling inadequate, unloved, and unappreciated. The indwelling presence of the Trinity and the merciful love offered us give us immense dignity and worth.

We ultimately have to accept the fact that we have been accepted all along. We cannot change that fundamental truth, no matter what we do. We always have a basis to begin again. The gift of grace requires us to receive it and allow it to sustain us.

Surrendering to that grace in our lives does not make us powerless and dependent. It actually energizes us with a surprising strength. Establishing a relationship with that Presence met deep within our lives changes us. Prayer is that activity which helps us give space to the working of grace. An interior life of attentiveness and receptivity to God not only gives us strength to carry out our desires, but it actually changes what we want. Our desires are transformed to be more and more in accord with God's desire for us and for all creation. Sometimes this change has been called "divinization", or a participation in God's knowing and loving. Our humanity reaches its high point in just such a profound union.

18

PRINCIPLES OF IMMIGRATION

"I was a stranger, and you welcomed me."
(Mt 25: 35)

The Catholic bishops of the United States discussed immigration in a pastoral statement, *Welcoming the Stranger Among Us*. This document, written in 2000, remains relevant. It discusses three basic principles regarding immigration:

1. People have the right to migrate to sustain their lives and the lives of their families.

2. A country has a right to regulate its borders and control immigration.

3. A country must regulate its borders with justice and mercy.

People Have a Right to Migrate

Immigrants are attempting to escape poverty and to flee violence. They are seeking safety and an opportunity to provide for their families. Most of our families have come to this country for similar reasons. We realize we are a nation founded on immigrants.

The Bishops are clear that immigration is not necessarily something to be celebrated. It usually means that conditions in the home country are deteriorating. Those who migrate to another country usually are desperate for a better life and more humane opportunities. In an ideal world, the community of nations would help countries develop conditions which would make emigration unnecessary.

Countries have a Right to Regulate Immigration and Control Borders

While individuals have the right to move to other countries for a safe and humane life, no country is required to accept all people who wish to enter. No country has the obligation to receive so many immigrants that its social and economic life are jeopardized.

Because a country has the right, and the need, to regulate its borders and control immigration, the Bishops caution against seeing such control as evil or negative. Those whose work it is to enforce our country's immigration laws are serving the common good. They do understand, and generally have compassion for, the unfortunate people who arrive at our borders looking for a better life.

A Country Must Regulate Its Borders with Justice and Mercy

Catholic social justice teaching has two fundamental principles: the absolute equality of all people, and commitment to the common good. Whether documented or undocumented, a person has a right to have basic human needs met: food, shelter, clothing, education, and health care. The Gospel warns us that the rich man cannot ignore the poor man, Lazarus, who sits at the gate. A country simply cannot turn its back on all who come to its borders, and care only for its own citizens.

Humane and just treatment involves keeping families together. A merciful policy will not force separations. To criminalize the mere attempt to immigrate is immoral. Nor will a merciful policy allow individuals to live and work productively for years in the country without the opportunity to become citizens. Such a policy is against the common good, and it is against basic justice.

Pope Francis and Today's Crisis

Pope Francis, who has shown a special concern for migrants, continues to speak to the importance of the issue. In his latest apostolic exhortation, Gaudete and Exsultate, he is critical of those who minimize the situation of migrants. He writes, for a Christian, "the only proper attitude is to stand in the shoes of those brothers and sisters of ours who risk their lives to offer a future to their children. Can we not realize that this is exactly what Jesus demands of us, when he tells us that in welcoming the stranger we welcome him" *(cf. Mt 25, 35)*?

Certainly, immigration policies have to take into consideration political, economic, and other pragmatic realities. But these policies need to be compassionate and humane, and just. No one wants to hear the Lord say, "I was a stranger, and you did not welcome me."

19

TWO ESSENTIALS IN LIFE
Meaning and Community

Meaning

Having checked all the boxes in life, such as education, job, family, house, security, we often find one box still unfilled: meaning, or spirituality. We join organizations, and have memberships, even in churches. But in the end, an elusive 'something more' haunts us.

To acknowledge the hunger and realize a yearning yet unfulfilled is the beginning of another journey in life. And it is not something we do; it is something given us, a path we find ourselves traveling. Call it a more whole or deeper life, or a more mature spirituality. We don't make that journey willingly or easily. Usually, something seriously disrupts the controlled life we have been struggling to keep together.

For a Christian, this departure from habits and routines begins with an experience of grace, of a realization that we are loved, without merit. We don't see grace, or necessarily feel this love, but in events, relationships, or whatever else has happened, we spontaneously know we have been blessed. And this blessing calls our restless heart to respond, to want to know more about this call, this invitation, this 'vocation.'

The love of God always calls us into a fuller humanity, a wider freedom, a deeper relationship. This path has no guideposts, no maps. It is a journey into the 'beyond-the-graspness of God.' It calls for surrender and trust. Cardinal Newman, a recently canonized convert to Catholicism, famously told of his experience in a poem. In part, it reads:

> Lead, Kindly Light, amidst th'encircling gloom,
> Lead Thou me on!
> The night is dark, and I am far from home,
> Lead Thou me on!
> Keep Thou my feet; I do not ask to see
> The distant scene; one step enough for me.
> I was not ever thus nor prayed that
> Thou shouldst lead me on;
> I love to choose and see my path; but now
> Lead Thou me on!

Community

A deeper, more mature spirituality does not lead into isolation, but into community. Staying on the surface of my life, trying to keep it together, leads to individualism and isolation. An acknowlegement of my need for a strength beyond myself joins me with all men and women who have to wait in hope for God's mercy. With St. Paul we can hear the Lord say, "My grace is sufficient for you" *(2 Cor 12, 9)*. The realization is that it is all gift, that we have been loved so that we, in turn, may love; we have been gifted, so we, in turn, may gift.

Isolation and loneliness abound in our world. Another convert to Catholicism, Dorothy Day, opened up her heart to the homeless, the poor, the left out, the hungry, and she founded numerous homes for the gathering of God's beloved people. At the end of her autobiography, The Long Loneliness, she wrote:

> We cannot love God unless we love each other, and to love we must know each other. We know Him in the breaking of bread, and we know each other in the breaking of bread, and we are not alone any more. Heaven is a banquet and life is a banquet, too, even with a crust, where there is companionship.
>
> We have all known the long loneliness and we have learned that the only solution is love and that love comes with community.

Day was feeding more than empty stomachs. She was giving nourishment to broken spirits. When Pope Francis challenged the church to be like a field hospital, he was pointing to a wounded and broken people who are in need of triage. We all share brokenness and wounds. Among the deepest wounds are a lack of meaning in life, and an absence of companionship in community. Each of our lives can be a witness to meaning found in a relationship with the Lord. Each of our lives, in some way, can be a shelter for those needing connection and companionship.

20

CARRY YOUR BURDEN, AND MINE TOO!

"Most of us carry a heavier burden than the rest of us realize." I have often thought about the truth of this observation. But, not only do people carry heavy burdens, we often ask them to carry our burden as well. One time in a meeting I heard one man describe another in rather negative terms. Those of us listening had the same thought: "He's actually describing himself!" It is a simple dynamic to witness. One person finds fault in another, without realizing it is her own fault, or at least, she shares the same fault.

Jesus observed the same dynamic. When you are about to criticize another for having a "splinter" in the eye, you had better first look at the "log" in your own. He also warned the men judging the adulterous woman to examine their own virtue first. It is too easy to let another carry our "sins" for us.

Projection

We often project onto another what we do not acknowledge in ourselves. If we are controlling, we blame another for being controlling. In order to avoid coming to terms with our own weakness, we ask another to carry it. We are then absolved. It is the other person's fault, and we can criticize it in them. Although we are aware of the possibility of projection, it is amazing how often we are unaware when it is happening.

A clue to projection is extreme or inappropriate emotion. When a reaction is out of all proportion to what caused it, it is possible projection is present. It may be that the other person is not entirely innocent, but they are being painted far worse than they really are. They may have "hooks" or aspects which catch or invite the projection. I hang the story of my life on those "hooks" and fight it out there. I am creating the other person in my own image. I am not allowing them to be themselves.

Shadow

The most dangerous time of the day, speaking metaphorically, can be high noon. When I live fully in the bright sunshine, and have no visible shadow, I can fool myself. I can believe that I have no "shadow" side, no unacknowledged negative or unintegrated part of my personality.

How many times have we seen someone who, in their righteousness, zealously denounced the sins of others and then tragically fall from grace themselves. Saint Teresa of Avila warned her sisters about having too much indiscreet zeal. She said we can learn from those who shock us. A good rule of thumb may be that where there is a constellation of high ideals and virtuous living, there is also the greater possibility of a hidden shadow.

From one psychologist's point of view, sin is "a refusal to come to consciousness." The simple act of awareness changes the situation. By becoming aware of what we have been doing we then can begin to own something that has been hidden or deflected to another. Once we own it, we can begin to withdraw it from the other person. It is not just a matter of greater insight. The experience of my own brokenness and need for healing and forgiveness can be a surprising cross. But it is also the path to a greater openness to a compassionate God.

Social Sin

Projection can be dangerous when entire groups deny their dark side, and find others to blame. Often, the majority in the land projects onto the minority. The majority blame the minority for evils they are not comfortable owning themselves. The minority are blamed for being violent and destructive. The less we know about another, the easier it is to paint them according to our need. Immigrants can be inviting targets for projection.

Jesus dealt with many if the "shadow" figures of his time. He mingled with, and ate meals with, those whom others considered outcasts, unworthy members of society. They were convenient scapegoats for the "good" religious persons. A truly Christian community is not noted for perfection; it is noted for compassion, forbearance, forgiveness, and a willingness to begin again. It has room for an honest acceptance of shadow.

May Jesus' followers humbly be aware of their own continuing need for vigilance and forgiveness. And may they stand by those who are unfairly made to carry others' burdens.

PART TWO

An Interior Life

21

A SIMPLE WAY TO PRAY

One of the complaints about spiritual writings is that much is written about the importance of prayer, but little is written about how to pray. And, often, prayer is presented as a complex process requiring a good deal of time.

Here is a description of prayer from the Little Flower, St. Thérèse of Lisieux, which implies a simple way of praying. For me, prayer is an aspiration of the heart, it is a simple glance directed heaven, it is a cry of gratitude and love in the midst of trial well as joy; finally it is something great, supernatural, which expands my soul and unites me to Jesus (*Story of a Soul*).

Notice, for the Little Flower, prayer is not simply thinking thoughts. It is a heartfelt, affective movement, a surge of the heart. And it may be a momentary movement. Walking down a corridor, looking up from a desk, waiting at a stoplight, the heart can leap to God. No complicated steps. No esoteric exercises. The prayer it suggests could be a simple, "Thank you!" or "Help!" or "Amen!", or a wordless moment of delight, wonder, or grief.

And this simple look is directed toward heaven. Heaven was the word that captured the whole point of life for Therese. It was the first word she could read. She would gaze at the stars, and one particular cluster appeared to form a "T." She pointed it out to her father, and told him her name was written in heaven. When she experienced good things in life, she said heaven would be like that, but without end. In other words, heaven is her expression for the place where the deepest desires of the human heart are fulfilled. Other hearts may have other expressions.

She says prayer is a cry of gratitude and love. There is something right in this surge, this cry. It is honest, true, and flung into the universe on the wings of hope. The one who prays intuitively knows, or truly hopes, that this prayer is honest. Not only is the direction of the prayer a mystery; the source or origin of the prayer is also a question. Is someone else praying in my prayer? We do believe the Holy Spirit is praying in us. There is something right and true in this honest expression of feeling.

It is a prayer embracing both trial and joy. The cry comes from our daily experience in life. It may express the joy of a simple accomplishment or outcome; it may express the frustration of a momentary difficulty, or the experience of being in a dark place in life. But, the cry can also arise from a powerful sense of the graciousness of life, unrelated to any specific reason. This prayer is simple and powerful, as is the young Saint herself!

22

THE VALUE OF SILENCE

The beginnings of this particular religious Order were not recorded for history. The first members had little inclination to keep records. The beginnings were later imaginatively reconstructed. In the reconstructed story the first community was described in idyllic terms, with an emphasis on silence.

The monks were so peacefully disposed to each other that there was no disunity among them. In their speech they were armed with silence, for there was no garrulousness among them. And because of this they were peaceful and self-assured: their heart did not accuse them before God.

The Book of the First Monks

Though the actual conditions of the first community were lost in the mists of time, the imagined conditions instruct us in the value the Order placed on silence.

Monks prefer quiet environments. At a very basic level, silence lessens the chance of misunderstanding, offending, distracting, or any of the many other problems speech may cause. The monks were peaceful because no one was expressing anger or other emotions which may create drama. The monks were peaceful because "there was no garrulousness among them."

Silence is not simply the absence of noise. If that is all it is, it is the silence of the grave. Silence, for the monks, was a weapon, a defense against the enemies of their life, those noises which would distort their life. The monks, therefore, were "armed with silence." Disturbances in the environment can unsettle an interior life.

Of course, most of us live in the monastery of the world, where silence may be at a premium. Still, times of silence can eventually help us be a person who values silence. Our silence conditions our speech. It helps us choose our words carefully, weighing what we say. We can restrain ourselves, speaking when it is appropriate, and saying no more than is appropriate.

At night, silence descends on a monastery. The experience of night, in its many forms, speaks of the mystery of the world, and the nearness of God. It is a time of patient waiting, keeping vigil and looking for the first faint rays of dawn. "Very early when the sun had risen…they came to the tomb" (Mark 16, 2). It is all expectation, awaiting the arrival of the Lord in our life.

Silence in the day is not simply a quieter time than night. During the day, silence is meant to accompany all that we do; it is a deep listening for, and attending to, God's quiet presence. In time, the one who has interiorized silence and listened for God's approach, will more and more live in a way cooperative with the reign of God.

My silence gives me a chance to hear who I truly am. Silence may take me below my usual banter and pronouncements and allow a deeper self to emerge. The self I meet includes the wounded and broken self I neglect. This self needs to be welcomed and exposed to the mercy of God. But it is truer to who I am, and so gives me peace.

My silence also allows another to be who she or he is. My silence keeps me from describing or painting another person according to my ideas, my projections. My silence allows another to speak her truth. Silence allows both of us to come into our own. Speech that comes out of silence is careful not to insult another in his presence, nor harm another in her absence. Because they were not "garrulous" the monks in the imagined community "were peaceful and self-assured; their heart did not accuse them before God."

Many practices are important for engaging the world. Among them, the practice of silence can add quality and depth to life. In the quiet I may come to realize my true poverty and my total dependence on God. This contemplative awareness allows me to be in solidarity with all who wait. "Your strength will be in silence and hope" (Isaiah 30, 15).

23

THE DESERT

It has been many years since I first saw the film, "Lawrence of Arabia." What has remained with me are images of a vast desert and the small human caravans or columns attempting to navigate it. Panoramic scenes of the desert were exhilarating, but threatening at the same time. This desert did not seem to be a place to live in, but to pass through, hopefully in safety.

Our story of faith includes interludes in the desert. The Jewish people traveled from slavery to freedom through the desert. Real deserts and metaphorical deserts have been part of the Christian story since John the Baptist went into the desert to prepare a path for the Lord. Jesus went out into the desert and struggled with temptation. Hermits and monks withdrew to isolated places to be with the Lord. Individuals have gone to deserts, caves, or mountains as they discerned God's will for them. From such settings emerged numerous religious orders, reformers of the church, and ordinary holy Christians.

What is it about the "desert"? Solitude and silence immediately come to mind. The desert has a basic landscape and simplicity of arrangement. It lacks clutter, and so provides for clear vision. It is not a natural home for us, and so we are vulnerable in the desert. Life may be seen in its most basic form. Priorities and assumptions may rise to awareness for examination. The desert can be a temporary or liminal experience as we undergo personal transformations.

Desert Times

Some deserts we choose to enter. Groups and individuals make retreats or have "days of recollection" in order to step back and examine life. Those entering religious life will spend desert time in a novitiate, a place and period of time which replicates many of the conditions of the desert. They will have space and quiet for reflection, guided by directors. Distractions are kept to a minimum. Here it is hard to run from oneself.

The Church has an entire season devoted to a desert experience. Lent is a time of purification of heart and mind in preparation for the celebration of the Lord's Resurrection, and our own transformation into Christ. The lengthy season and the powerful scripture readings invite us to enter a time of reflection and awareness. The traditional exercises are prayer, almsgiving, and fasting.

Other deserts are unbidden. Times of illness, serious loss, stress, setbacks, can all be times of wandering in a desert of confusion and hurt. In these times we are vulnerable, and perhaps more open to seeing the truth of our lives. The clarity of a desert experience lets us see our brokenness. Our automatic assumptions and responses are challenged. Perhaps we realize how unfree we are to change.

Rules for the Desert

Spiritual guides recommend:

Travel light. We are trying to attend to God in the moment, and not be preoccupied.

Lessen self-reliance. Otherwise we may forget we need God.

Be available. We are not searching for God. God will find us.

Fast so as not to be full. When we are full we may not know our deeper hunger for God.

Keep vigil. Prayer now is more listening than speaking.

Share with others. It helps them, and keeps us from being self-absorbed.

With clarity also comes an awareness of our blessed condition. In the desert we may see the Lord's approach and hear the Lord's words of compassion and mercy. Surrendering to God in faith lets our desert become a garden.

24

A HEALING PRESENCE

When Jesus saw the crowds coming to him, he saw a people who were "sick." He referred to himself as a physician who has come to heal. He did speak of judgment and he strongly condemned sin. But when confronted with an individual sinner, his words and actions conveyed mercy. He did not play the role of the judge who has come to chastise the sinner.

It is difficult to find an occasion when Jesus criticized or condemned an individual. He was critical of groups such as religious leaders who were righteous and who burdened their followers. But when it came to an individual, whether tax collector or prostitute, he did not harangue. He deeply understood their situation and responded accordingly.

To Zacchaeus the tax collector who eagerly climbed a tree to see him, he said, "Zacchaeus, come down… Today salvation has come to this house." To the woman who was brought before him as an adulterer, and whose accusers drifted away because of their own guilt, he said, "Neither do I condemn you."

Jesus showed little interest in belittling an individual by moralizing or lecturing. He did not ask that they grovel, nor did he rehearse their past. He only asked that they have sorrow for their sins, and then go forward in their lives trusting in a merciful God.

Jesus acted as the father who raced to welcome his prodigal son, not waiting for the son to come all the way to the father's house. The father had no need to hear the wayward son's anguished speech of self-recrimination. The father had no punishing conditions for the son's return. He offered loving acceptance and an invitation to the feast.

It is not that Jesus exonerated people. Sin and guilt were present. So were sorrow and regret. In the light of the reign of God our sins are exposed. But Jesus had no need to burden the already burdened. He was treating the sickness that underlies the deeds. He was healing the wound, the hurt, the brokenness that led to self-centered and destructive behavior.

Jesus, the physician, healed the blind, the lame, the mute, the possessed. The Gospels tell too many stories with too many witnesses to deny He truly healed people. And he need not have skirted the laws of matter. It is possible that Jesus, often with few words and even fewer gestures, evoked the healing power that resides in the depth of matter, demonstrating the potential of our graced world. Jesus' presence and a person's faith often were a powerful combination resulting in "mighty deeds."

Physical healings pointed to the presence of the reign of God, the reign that was central to Jesus' preaching. The deeper healing of God's presence mended hearts and spirits, and made them inwardly whole and free, and available to God. Once I met a man who was wheelchair-bound. People from his parish regularly gathered around him to pray for his healing. He said, "Father, they often pray like this, and I have been trying to tell them, I was healed a long time ago!"

If Jesus was a healer, can we His Church be any less a healing presence in the world? Kindness and compassion go a long way in mending hearts and minds, and sometimes even bodies. Simple accepting presence, and a willingness to understand people from their point of view can calm anxious lives and lessen fear. Pope Francis is reminding the Church that Jesus accompanied the poor and the lost. He loved them into health.

We can all find ourselves in that company. With faith in the healing presence of Jesus, we are free to acknowledge the truth of our lives and confess our sins. And we too can humbly ask to be healed. "Go your way," said Jesus. "Your faith has saved you."

25

THE SEVEN CAPITAL SINS
Are They Relevant Today?

The classic seven capital sins are pride, envy, anger, sloth, avarice, gluttony, and lust. Worried about a weakened sense of sin, some Catholics believe we need such a list to identify sinful behavior. Over time our consciences may become dull and we excuse ourselves when we should be accusing ourselves. Periodically, lists of sins are created to remind us to stay alert.

Listing sins was begun by eastern monks to identify actions harmful to monastic life. Pope Gregory the Great (d. 604) believed these sins were applicable to all Christians; his list numbered eight. St. Thomas Aquinas collapsed pride and vainglory to establish the seven capital sins we know today.

Pope Gregory called them "capital" because certain sins are major. Thomas Aquinas (d. 1274) called them capital because they are the source or fountainhead of sinful behaviors (caput is Latin for "head"). The "seven" are not necessarily sins but more like tendencies or dispositions which may underlie specific sinful actions. A recent survey by U.S. Catholic magazine found that 74% of respondents agreed that the seven capital sins are still a helpful guide in determining how to live our lives.

The "Seven"

The seven capital sins provide a basis for assessing the spiritual life of a Christian. They name subtle faults of the good person. Here are condensed descriptions drawing on traditional and contemporary sources:

Pride

We take undue credit for what is gift from God. This sin can hide in the disguise of good. We can be proud of our humility. We can downplay our faults, and smugly compare ourselves with others. We take the last place in order to be first in others' estimation. It is amazing how our ego can insert itself in even the most altruistic endeavors and make it about "us."

Envy

When others are praised for their goodness, we are sad. The accomplishments and abilities of others may threaten us. Rather than being happy for them, we feel a judgment on ourselves. By excessive moralizing and criticizing of others, we diminish them and thereby elevate ourselves.

Anger

We become impatient and angry with ourselves because of our moral failures. We expect more satisfaction from our religious practices. We become angry with others on whom we project our own shortcomings. As years advance we become bitter and more selfish, perhaps complaining that life has been unfair.

Sloth

Our standard for judgment is whether or not we are pleased or satisfied. If we are pleased with ourselves, so is God. We put off dealing with moral issues in our life, such as forgiving others or establishing a practice of prayer. We excuse ourselves from a deeper maturity and a more vibrant Christian life. We may engage in hard work in order to evade inner work.

Avarice (Greed)

It is difficult to be satisfied with less because we usually want more, material as well as spiritual possessions. We may multiply religious practices hoping to have greater consolation. An accumulation of things, even money, may be less important than the greed to be recognized and admired.

Gluttony

The hunger we have is ultimately for God, but it is easy for our heart to mistake the good things of God for God; we become addicted to them. We lose control and lack sobriety and temperance. We consume people and a multiplicity of experiences. Today we may lose ourselves in information and the technology conveying it. Thomas Merton warned about taking on too many commitments and concerns, thereby doing violence to oneself.

Lust

We love others for what they can do for us, rather than love them for their own good and God's intention. But we are not required to have a dead heart. The challenge for us is to have a pure heart, one free from possessiveness and clinging. Our sexual energy is not to be denied or suppressed but channeled in a mature expression energizing us and giving life to others.

The seven capital sins continue to name spiritual maladies which find expression in ever-changing contemporary concerns, such as economic injustice, substance abuse, and environmental pollution. Lists of sins should never obscure the abundance of God's grace. But, they should give us reason to humbly pray, "Lord, have mercy!"

26

EARNING GOD'S LOVE?

My mother often prayed with a holy card. The prayer was an expression of great trust in God, but, at the bottom of the card was printed, "Must be prayed before 11 am." I do not think my mother watched the clock, but whoever printed the card was expressing a need in all of us.

In other words, although we do trust in God's care for us, something in us needs to feel we have earned God's love. Most people will laugh at such directions. But, there is in us a strong tendency to secure our lives through our own efforts. We learned as children that if we play by the rules, and stay within the lines, we are loved. If we break the rules we are in trouble. And we carry that scorecard over into our relationship with God.

When we put more faith in our religious practices than in God's love, we are turning religion into bargaining. If I bury the statue upside down, I have a better chance of being heard! Practices can be an expression of faith, but they can be misused as bargaining chips.

Moralism to Christian Morality

It is very difficult for Catholics to shift from a moralism to true Christian morality. Moralism believes that we are punished for doing bad, and loved for doing good. Christian morality, however, maintains there is nothing we have to do to be loved by God. That love has been given us freely. God's love cannot be bartered for, or earned, or deserved. It is simply there, like the air we breathe.

And there is nothing we can do to lose or turn away that love. We may not believe in it, we may not accept it, we may walk away. But God never walks away from us. There is nothing we can do to turn God's love away. The story of humanity is God's faithfulness in the face of our faithlessness.

The abundance of God's love is difficult for us to fathom. Our sense of fairness is tested when Jesus tells how workers hired late in the day received the same wages as those hired early in the day. We want to quantify God's love and see it fairly portioned out, but God's love does not work according to our economies.

God's Merciful Love

The lives we try to live are in response to God's love; they are not an attempt to earn it. We are encouraged to let that love come into our lives and make a difference. We can be generous and confident with our lives because God has been generous with us.

Faith has been described as the acceptance, finally, of having been accepted all along. Such faith allows us to approach God without fear, without a sense of being unworthy. When we focus on our shortcomings, even our sins, we forget we are loved. To wallow in our sins in remorse can be overly self-centered. To get up and go on, confident in God's merciful love, centers life properly.

My novice master had a favorite passage from St. Paul's letter to the Romans: "It is not a question of the one who wills or exerts, but of God showing mercy" *(Rom 9:16)*. The true fulcrum in life is not our effort, but God's grace, by which we do what we do. When we first heard the novice master we were 18 years old, and sure of our strength. I have had the occasion to visit his grave in rural Pennsylvania, and there on his gravestone is, "It is not a question of the one who wills or exerts, but of God showing mercy." And I appreciate it much more.

27

MAKE AMERICA GOOD!

Serious and good-willed people are working to "Make America Great." We also need to make America good. Greatness without goodness is hollow. Greatness without goodness, will collapse on itself.

If making America great means recognizing and listening to the concerns of all sectors of the country; if it means having a healthy economy, and a safe and secure country; who could object!

However, making America great does not require causing division in the country. No definition of greatness calls for fraying our common bonds or denigrating particular groups.

Great Men and Women

My father worked 36 years for the United States government. Our family lived on a government base for ten years. Our neighbors were military families and the families of other civil service workers. My friends in those days were boys whose fathers were civilian and military, including one father who was a Lt. Colonel and another who was a General.

If any individuals in the country were among those who made America great, my father and his co-workers would have to be on the list. No one would accuse them of being unpatriotic or un-American. My dad even was critical of applauding the National Anthem. You listened to it respectfully, he said. They didn't call themselves great. They didn't have to. Their service to the country spoke for itself. Greatness was an assessment for others to make.

Great and Good

But, they also lived in a way that would make America good. Families on the base, both military and civilian, went to churches of various denominations. Our family went to St. Rose parish in Wilmington. My religious education continued at St. Raymond's parish in Joliet with the Franciscan sisters. We were taught the Sermon on the Mount, and the Beatitudes. The Gospels challenged us. Jesus taught, "Whoever wishes to be great among you shall be your servant" *(Mt 20, 26)*.

The officers on the base were formed by the principles and ethics they learned in the military. They knew, and their experience in other countries told them, America's greatness is in its values. One of the officers, Captain Carson, was the leader of our scout troop. In scouts we were guided by the Scout Oath: we promised to "do my duty to God and my country…to help other people at all times… "

Later, I lived many years in Washington, D.C. The documents maintained in the National Archives and the inscriptions on various monuments were an education in American values. While not perfect themselves, Washington, Jefferson, Lincoln, Roosevelt, Dr. King remind us of our higher aspirations. The issues of the country will be pursued, debated, and legislated. At the same time, this process can respect human rights and cultivate the common good. In addition to making America 'great', we also want to continue to make America good.

An amusing memory:

I was pacing up and down in a train station in Britain.

An elderly man, seated on a bench, had been watching me.

Finally, he said, "A Yank, eh?"

I said, "Yes, I'm a Yank."

"Some people don't like Yanks." he said, "But, I find they come in handy now and then."

28

THREE FEASTS IN OCTOBER

Among the many feasts in October, the liturgical calendar features two contemplative nuns and an itinerant friar. The two nuns are St. Thérèse of Lisieux (October 1) and St. Teresa of Avila (October 15), and the friar is St. Francis of Assisi (October 4).

What do we learn from them? In sum, we learn to pray, to witness and to trust.

St. Teresa of Avila

St. Teresa of Avila defined prayer to be, "nothing else than an intimate sharing between friends; it means taking time frequently to be alone with Him who we know loves us." Sometimes this prayer is described as conversation with a friend. Notice the lack of fear in her understanding. Prayer is a relationship of trust. Teresa said we cannot know God unless we know ourselves; but we cannot know ourselves unless we know God. The more she could say "God" in her life, the more she could say "Teresa."

The purpose of prayer, she taught, was to be in conformity with God's will. In our prayer we are changed. More and more we want what God wants. As this friendship with God deepens, the one who prays lives in accord with the Gospel. She witnesses to a world that is more peaceful and just, a non-violent world where the immense dignity of each individual is acknowledged.

The only terminal problem, in Teresa's estimation, is to stop praying.

St. Francis of Assisi

St. Francis practiced the Gospels. His imitation of Christ was literal. If Jesus met and touched lepers, so did Francis. If Jesus took to the road to announce the present and coming reign of God, so did Francis. Jesus' disciples were sent to towns without gold or silver, no second tunic, or other provisions. Francis' followers similarly were to travel lightly, taking only what was essential for their mission.

Francis did not want his disciples to simply talk about the Christian life; he wanted them to perform the Gospel. Do what Jesus did. They were to preach by their witness. Words were to be used only "if necessary." They were to demonstrate what Christian life looked like, in effect saying, "See, this is how it is done!"

Pope Francis, the first Pope to choose the name of the poor friar, also speaks of witnessing to the Gospel. Instead of attempting to convert others, Pope Francis wants the Christian community to grow by attraction. People are not often impressed with words; they are impressed by a person's manner of living.

St. Thérèse of Lisieux

When Thérèse began to write an account of her life, *The Story of a Soul*, she said she was "singing the mercies of the Lord." And she quoted St. Paul, "So then there is a question not of him who wills nor of him who runs, but of God showing mercy" *(Rom 9: 16)*. Pope St. John Paul II, in declaring Thérèse a Doctor of the Universal Church, said, "She helped to heal souls of the rigors and fears of Jansenism, which tended to stress God's justice rather than his divine mercy."

Sometimes called the little way, Thérèse's spirituality was not a retreat from accomplishments in life, but an encouragement to go forward with absolute confidence and trust in God's merciful love. Thérèse had her share of sorrows, including physical suffering and challenges to her faith. Nonetheless, she declared, "Everything is a grace!"

Bishop Patrick Ahern summed-up Thérèse's little way; "It is a school of self-acceptance, which goes beyond accepting who you are, to wanting to be who you are. It is a way of coming to terms with life, not as it might be, but as it is."

29

SACRED PLACES

Pope Francis, in his prophetic letter on care for our planet, wrote, "The history of our friendship with God is always linked to particular places which take on an intensely personal meaning; we all remember places, and revisiting those memories does us much good" *(Laudato Si)*.

Most of us probably have special places we remember. Childhood places may stand out in memory. Places of vacation, retreat, and pilgrimage often leave us with lasting memories. Perhaps the beauty of nature, such as a mountain, lake, forest or desert, enhances our memory. And in certain places, for reasons largely unknown to us, we may experience the presence of the Holy.

But special places are not always remote and scenic. The Trappist monk, Thomas Merton, remembered an epiphany he had one day on a street corner in Louisville, Kentucky. He wrote, "In Louisville, at the corner of Fourth and Walnut, in the center of the shopping district, I was suddenly overwhelmed with the realization that I loved all these people, that they were mine and I theirs, that we could not be alien to one another even though we were total strangers" *(Conjectures of a Guilty Bystander)*.

Not all experiences of the holy are instantaneous. Some experiences are the result of time and familiarity. An oratory, grotto, chapel, or church may not initially affect us in any special way. But, after many experiences of entering the space for prayer or attending many sacramental celebrations, the place becomes 'holy' for us. The space itself may be ordinary in its appearance, but familiarity with it through numerous occasions of prayer and celebration makes it a comfortable and healing space. We are at home here, and we are ourselves, and God is near.

A Graced World

Pope Francis reminds us that every part of creation gives praise to God by being itself. And because we live in a graced world, any part of creation may speak of God's loving presence. With such a 'sacramental imagination' the world lights up. It becomes a type of sacrament for us. "Nothing is profane for those who know how to see" *(Teilhard de Chardin).*

The 13th century Franciscan theologian John Duns Scotus wrote about the 'thisness' of things. *Haecceity* he called it (*haec*, Latin for 'this'). Through 'this' particular place I enter into the spaciousness of God's creation. A contemporary Franciscan writer concludes, "go deep in any one place and you will meet all places."

To appreciate the sanctity of our daily life we sometimes have to go away… and then come back. The poet T.S. Eliot wrote, "… the end of all our exploring will be to arrive where we started and know the place for the first time" *(Four Quartets).* Then we may see the sacred depth of our days.

Re-visiting a place, or its memories, does not guarantee another experience of the divine. We cannot summon the experience of God. And our faith does not rely on having 'experiences'. We do not travel by sight, as St Paul reminds us, but by faith. But, now and then, our faith is renewed as we remember or re-visit a place where God's presence was palpable.

The truth is we are always experiencing God, usually implicitly. Special places help sensitize us to God's presence even in less numinous places. For St. Teresa of Avila, God's presence was also 'among the pots and pans.' To be aware of God's presence in our ordinary lives is a cause for praise and thanksgiving. Pope Francis reminds us to be grateful for the special places that light up our lives. These sacred places are way stations on our pilgrimage of faith!

30

CHRISTMAS
A Feast of Presence and Love

Celebrating the birth of Christ is a timely reminder that we are not alone, and that we are loved. In these days, when so many people report loneliness and anxiety, Christmas is a feast of presence and love.

We Are Not Alone

Loneliness is a common condition in our time. We have never had greater ability to communicate with others, but many people today report feeling lonely. And when we do not have meaningful contact with others, and are essentially isolated, our mental health can be affected.

Christmas means that God chose to accompany us in life. The Lord did not have an uncomplicated life. Plans went awry; followers fled; days alternated between success and rejection. When we look on Gethsemane and the Cross we realize how fully God entered our human experience. Christmas tells us our God is with us, Emmanuel.

We are never truly alone, although we may not always experience God's presence. People of faith often report experiencing a 'dark night,' a time of loss of consolation when God seems to be absent. But they continue to believe with patience, perseverance, and trust. God can be a compassionate presence hidden within an experience of absence.

Jesus called on his Father in moments of solitude, and taught his followers to pray. Prayer helps nurture a relationship with the Lord who is always with us. St. Augustine observed that, while God is with us, we are not always with God. Prayer is the key to establishing that relationship. The God revealed to us by Jesus is a presence in our lives, closer to us than we are to ourselves.

The Beloved of God

Who are we essentially? We are the beloved of God. That is our core identity and nothing can change it. We did not earn it. It was given us freely, unconditionally. No matter what we think about ourselves, no matter what people say about us, we are the beloved of God. God chose to be with us out of love for us, God's creation. "In this is love: not that we have loved God, but that he loved us…" *(1 Jn 4: 10)*.

Trusting that we are loved may be a life-long challenge. At times in life, we may wonder about love. Who loves us? Who or what gives our lives meaning? Much of our effort in life is an attempt to find answers to these questions. We think we are looking for something attainable in this world. But, we are warned by St. Augustine that these questions will only be answered finally and fully in relationship with God. Augustine acknowledged, "Our hearts are restless until they rest in Thee."

Christmas may sharpen our feelings of loneliness and isolation. But it may also be a celebration where we are reminded, often through family and friends, that we are not alone, and that we are truly loved. Christmas challenges us to find ways of linking up with others, for our sake and for theirs. Making connections and leaving space for God's presence, can happen in most forms of community. It is important for us to try to form loving relationships and trusting communities.

Quiet joy, deep reverence, and a peaceful atmosphere mark the scene in Bethlehem. Our deepest desires respond to this scene. Something in us says, "Yes! This is the way life should be." Celebrating Christmas is an act of hope! Our hope is grounded on the Lord's promise of an everlasting presence and love.

31

SUMMING UP THE YEAR OF MERCY

Last year, in his letter *Misericordiae Vultus*, Pope Francis called for a Jubilee Year of Mercy beginning in December. He declared, "Mercy is the very foundation of the church's life." Here is one list of take-aways from the year.

- The year of mercy arrived as a breath of fresh air, blowing through a church that at times has been judgmental and severe.

- This special year was anticipated early in the pontificate of Pope Francis. His response, "Who am I to judge?" set a new tone, welcomed by many individuals and communities within the church.

- Mercy is not simply one theme among many in the Gospel. Mercy is at the heart of the Gospel.

- Mercy expresses God's core identity. Mercy is the primary ingredient in God's relationship with us.

- The theme of a merciful God is a corrective to a narrow focus on justice. Sin remains a reality, as do judgment and justice. But mercy is the way God's justice is expressed.

- The Pope challenged church leaders, and all of us, to be "ministers of mercy." Jesus did not condemn the woman accused of adultery. We are not to "stone" people with the law.

- Parishes went to great efforts to make the Sacrament of Reconciliation available, and large numbers of the faithful took advantage of the opportunity.

- Pope Francis' exhortation on marriage and family, *Amoris Laetitia*, demonstrated a sensitivity to the complexity of modern relationships. He encouraged an adult church, one in which members prayerfully followed their conscience.

- In his encyclical on the environment, *Laudato Si*, Pope Francis wrote about his namesake Saint Francis who "shows us just how inseparable the bond is between concern for nature, justice for the poor, commitment to society and interior peace."

Works of Mercy

- One of the stated goals of the year of mercy was to awaken consciences too often dulled in the face of poverty.

- We were reminded of St. John Paul II's encyclical on mercy, *Dives in Misericordia*, where he said those who have experienced the mercy of God are expected to practice mercy toward others.

In particular, Pope Francis has been challenging us to listen to the needs of the poor, to assist those who are on the peripheries of life.

- The works of mercy were placed front and center as an agenda for the jubilee year, and going forward.

- We were reminded of the corporal works of mercy to feed the hungry, give drink to the thirsty, clothe the naked, welcome the stranger, heal the sick, visit the imprisoned, and bury the dead.

- The canonization of Mother Teresa of Calcutta provided for the church and the world a challenging icon of mercy. She served "the poorest of the poor."

- The Saint did not always expect to heal or keep from dying those brought into her homes, but in their suffering and dying they would be welcomed, and treated with dignity; in their last hours they would know tender care.

- Mother Teresa also witnessed to the spiritual works of mercy: counseling, instructing, admonishing, comforting, forgiving, and praying.

- It is more than a matter of food and drink. She reminded us regularly,

> people not only hunger for bread but for love;
>
> people are thirsting for kindness, for compassion, for delicate love;
>
> the greatest disease is to be unwanted, unloved;
>
> people are hungry for God.

This jubilee year of mercy has been a commentary on the Gospel: "Be merciful just as your Father is merciful" *(Lk 6: 36)*.

32

THE PRACTICES OF LENT

Lent offers a time to live differently. Perhaps we have been locked into routines for most of the year. We have a chance to review and re-order our lives. It is a time for an honest appraisal. We may not have been as attentive to God as we would have liked. We honestly admit our failures and sins. We ask for a spirit of repentance and renewal.

Lent is a time to catch ourselves in our scatteredness. Perhaps our many concerns in life have left us without a center. We may live in a distracted, fragmented, even dissipated, way. Or, we may have been overly involved with ourselves to the neglect of others, and the Other.

Recommended practices in Lent are prayer, fasting, almsgiving. We can add vigils, reading scripture, and keeping silent. These time-honored practices are to help us have "purity of heart." A pure heart is a heart free to listen to God, and respond. It is a heart unencumbered with false idols and debilitating attachments. A traditional motto in the spiritual life is vacare deo, to be free for God

Lent is an opportunity to once more give attention to having an interior life. An interior life is a life centered on God. It is a life of awareness, reflection, openness. We enter the chapel of the heart and there keep vigil. Prayer is essentially listening to God, awaiting God's arrival. All of our words are an attempt to say the one word which is God's. In silence and expectation, we live in hope. This contemplative prayer leads to a purity of heart, and apostolic love.

In Lent we are encouraged to fast, so we will not be full. Many things in life can "fill" us. And being overstuffed, we no longer know our deeper hunger. Only God is sufficient food for that hunger. Fasting from what fills us also sensitizes us to our brothers and sisters who go without.

We give alms because God has been generous with us, and we are sent to share God's goodness with others. A deepening faith results in a growing generosity. Lent gives us a time to look around our lives and recognize those whom we are neglecting, those who may be on the periphery of our awareness, and in need.

Fundamentally, we are trying to learn how to love. The purpose of a pure heart is to be available for love. It has been said that the most profound way of loving God is to allow God to love us. That sounds doable, but actually it is difficult, principally because of the implications in accepting that love. St. Thérèse of Lisieux observed that God is not looking for people to punish; God is looking for people who will open their lives to God's transforming love. She judged that few there are who actually want to be this vulnerable, this trusting.

Conversion in Lent is to allow ourselves to be porous to God's love. It is a process of discerning the voice of God in the noise of life, allowing the Spirit to lead us where we would not go. It is a process of hearing the demands of the Gospel, with special attention to those left out.

God does not love us because we do good things; we do good things because God loves us, and God is good! With the psalmist we pray, "Create in me a pure heart, O God, and renew a steadfast spirit within me" *(Ps 51: 12).*

33

TIME TO DECLUTTER?

Periodically, we decide we need to get our life in order. We resolve to simplify, prioritize, declutter. A simple life attracts us.

Working against simplicity are the demands of modern living, and the desires of our heart. Our responsibilities may be multiple, demands on our time may be many, and the lure of increased income, a prominent reputation, a growing pride make simple living difficult. Money, status, possessions are always alluring.

Lifestyle gurus have plenty of advice. They encourage us to better organize, and even get rid of, some of the stuff of our lives. They challenge us to distinguish what we may want from what we truly need.

Clutter occurs not only in our outer environment, but we may also have inner clutter. Our interior life may experience storms of emotions and multiple concerns. We may feel pulled and distracted, anxious and restless. We may experience a need to declutter inwardly even as we get our outer life in order.

While simplifying life may be psychologically healthy, it may be spiritually helpful as well. Our faith tells us God is continually coming toward us, inviting us more fully into a life-giving relationship. Can God find us in the clutter of our life?

The Issue is Freedom

It is not necessarily a matter of having much or having little. Messy environments or packed schedules in themselves may not be a problem. The issue is freedom. Do we live in a way that makes us free to hear God in our life? Can God find us in the clutter of our life, or are we hidden from God? Do our commitments, cares, schedules so preoccupy us that we are simply not available to God?

A story is told in our Carmelite tradition about a friar who had a simple cross made out of blessed palm, and held together by a pin. For ten years he carried this cross with him wherever he went. His superior, St John of the Cross, finally took the cross from him. St. John judged that the friar was putting more trust in this little possession than in God. It is not the value or amount of what we have, but our relationship to it. Does it make our heart unfree to be open to God's approach and call?

St. Ignatius of Loyola encouraged individuals who were making a decision in life to find a place of "indifference" regarding their options. In other words, rather than making choices based on momentary enthusiasms or biases, Ignatius counseled stepping back to a place of freedom, "indifference," in order to make a choice which may be more in accord with the action of God in one's life.

A Routine of Prayer

Spiritual writers recommend that we find a space of freedom in our lives where we reverently attend to the presence of God. In other words, have a routine of prayer.

Show up in prayer on a regular basis, thank God for blessings, call on God's grace for strength and perspective. Since God knows what we want and need, our prayer can also be silent, wordless. In this space of attention and reverence we are making ourselves available to God, and allowing God to find us. For a moment we are not hidden within the clutter of our lives.

St. Paul's travels were many and often arduous. His concerns for the new Christian communities are evident in his letters. Still, he arrived at a place of clarity and balance in his life. In any circumstance he knew the source of his strength. Paul wrote:

> I know indeed how to live in humble circumstances; I know also how to live with abundance. In every circumstance and in all things I have learned the secret of being well fed and of going hungry, of living in abundance and of being in need. I have the strength for everything through him who empowers me *(Phil 4:12, 13)*.

34

RESURRECTION
What Happened After Jesus Died on the Cross?

Our Christian faith hinges on belief in the Resurrection. "If Christ has not been raised," wrote St. Paul, " your faith is vain" *(1 Cor 15:17)*. The Resurrection was not an event able to be seen with human eyes. It defies our categories; our language is insufficient to fully explain the Resurrection.

Pope Benedict XVI writes in *Jesus of Nazareth*, "None of the evangelists recounts Jesus' Resurrection itself. It is an event taking place within the mystery of God between Jesus and the Father, which for us defies description: by its very nature it lies outside human experience." The Pope says the Resurrection "opens up a new dimension of human existence." No single explanation of the Resurrection fully captures the reality. No one saw it.

What we do see in the Bible is a record of encounters with the resurrected Christ. St. Paul's faith was born in a powerful encounter with Christ. Peter, too, experienced the resurrected Christ, as did the apostles, and a large number of Jesus' followers. An empty tomb, while in itself not proof of a resurrection, eventually played a part in the story circulating among early Christians. The very first to encounter the resurrected Christ was, most likely, Mary Magdalene. What did they experience? A physical body? An imaginary vision?

Two Explanations

One explanation today says that the visions of a resurrected Christ were born in the expectations of Jesus' followers. This explanation says that after Jesus' death, the intensity of the hopes and dreams of the disciples produced a vivid remembrance in their psyches. What they saw and heard was a product of their imagination.

However, standing in apparent opposition to that view, is the consistent conviction that Jesus' followers, after his death on the cross, encountered Jesus himself. They saw, heard, and touched him. But at first they did not recognize him.

The two views, that the disciples truly experienced Jesus after the Resurrection, and that the Jesus they saw were imaginative visions conditioned by their hopes and beliefs, are not necessarily opposed.

Our world is kept in existence by a God who continually creates. It is a world of grace, of divine presence. Something may have a natural explanation, and, at the same time, be a graced event, the result of God present in human processes and laws. Encounters with a resurrected Christ by Jesus' followers could be understood to be both the product of their deep desires to believe in Jesus, and the action of God. It is entirely a human work, and entirely a divine work. In their various visions, the disciples truly encountered the risen Lord.

The Effect of the Resurrection

The crucifixion seemed to negate Jesus' life and teaching. It dashed the hopes of his followers. The Resurrection re-affirmed all that Jesus taught, and confirmed the belief of those who had placed their hope in Him.

Perhaps the most telling evidence for the reality of the resurrection of Jesus is the powerful transformation in his followers. Whatever their description of the experience of the resurrected Christ, and the descriptions vary in the Gospels and in Acts, Jesus' followers were enabled to overcome their fears. They were emboldened to preach the Gospel, no matter what the consequences. Their witness, including martyrdom, quickly spread the faith throughout the Roman Empire.

The Resurrection means that the last word will always be God's word of life. No power, no darkness, no evil will ever be final. The Resurrection is the basis for the hope all Christians bring to their daily lives. The Paschal Mystery, the life, death, and resurrection of the Lord is the basic pattern of our lives, and the life of God's entire creation. Because of the Resurrection, the first Christians came to believe in Jesus as Lord and Savior.

35

FATHER MICHAEL McGIVNEY

"He was not a martyr, not a missionary, not a bishop, but a regular parish priest who lived that regular parish priesthood in an extraordinarily heroic way."

Fr. Walker, pastor of St. Mary Church, New Haven

Fr. Michael McGivney was a parish priest and Founder of the Knights of Columbus. On October 31, 2020, Fr. McGivney was beatified at the Cathedral of St. Joseph in Hartford, CT. He is now "Blessed Michael McGivney."

In a decree, Pope Francis praised Fr. McGivney for his "zeal for the proclamation of the Gospel and generous concern for his brothers and sisters." The Pope said Fr. McGivney was "an outstanding witness of Christian solidarity and fraternal assistance."

Cardinal Joseph Tobin of Newark represented Pope Francis and was principal celebrant at the beatification Mass. The Cardinal said, "Fr. McGivney's life is an illustration of how a holy priest can provide the necessary and intimate connection, so crucial in the life and mission of a parish. …The signature accomplishment for which he is remembered, founding the Knights of Columbus, grew out of his ministry as a parish priest."

Opening the door to the beatification of Fr. McGivney was a decree from Pope Francis recognizing as a miracle the healing of an unborn boy. The boy had fetal hydrops, a fatal accumulation of fluids in an unborn child. The healing was attributed to the intercession of Fr. McGivney. The boy, Michael "Mikey" Schachle, five years old, with Down syndrome, attended the beatification ceremony with his family. He walked up the aisle to bring a relic of Fr. McGivney to Cardinal Tobin.

A Son of Irish Immigrants

Fr. Michael McGivney was born and raised in Waterbury, CT. His parents, Patrick and Mary, were Irish immigrants. Michael was the eldest of thirteen children, six of whom died in infancy or childhood. He left school at thirteen to work in the spoon-making department of a brass mill. He entered the seminary at age sixteen.

Because French-speaking immigrants were coming into the Hartford diocese, and Bishop McFarland wanted priests better prepared to minister to them, McGivney was sent to study in Quebec, Niagara Falls, NY, and Montreal. However, when his father died, McGivney left the seminary to help his family.

McGivney resumed studies at St. Mary's Seminary in Baltimore, MD, and was ordained a priest on December 22, 1877, by Archbishop James Gibbons at the Baltimore Cathedral of the Assumption. Father McGivney's first assignment was to be curate in St. Mary's parish, New Haven, CT.

Knights of Columbus

McGivney was convinced that Catholic men needed some type of fraternal society. He saw how men often struggled to carry out their duties in life. And when the father of a family died, it was devastating to the family. In many cases, widows lived on in poverty.

McGivney, along with a small group of Irish-American parishioners, founded the Knights of Columbus. The Knights were to provide spiritual support for men, and in the event of a man's death, offer financial assistance to the widow and her children.

After considering various names for the new group, Knights of Columbus was chosen. In a time of tension between Catholics and the wider society, and suspicion about Catholics' loyalty to the Vatican, the choice of Columbus, a non-Gaelic name, signaled loyalty to the United States, and an openness to all nationalities.

The Knights of Columbus, now an international fraternal society, number more than 2 million members. The Knights generously support families and parishes, and carry out numerous charitable projects. They help where there is need.

Carl Anderson, Supreme Knight, said that Fr. McGivney anticipated Vatican II. His vision "empowered the laity to serve the Church and their neighbors in a new way, through a greater commitment to charity and build effective cooperation between laity and clergy." Anderson said that the beatification of Fr. McGivney will "encourage that vision of lay leadership and fellowship."

The Work of a Parish Priest

Conditions in the time of Father McGivney's ministry as a parish priest mirrored some of today's challenges. It was a time of few priests and many Catholics, resulting in multiple duties. It is thought that the hard work required to serve Catholic immigrant communities led to early deaths among priests. Diseases easily spread in those close communities. In the 1880's, for a parish priest, there was little hope of reaching fifty years of age and almost none of reaching seventy. Father Michael McGivney contracted influenza, leading to pneumonia. He died August 14, 1890, two days after his thirty-eighth birthday.

The beatification celebration emphasized Father McGivney's humility, his holy witness, and his love of the parishioners he served. Archbishop Leonard Blair of Hartford said, "I believe Fr. McGivney is truly Pope Francis' kind of priest. A model of his time of closeness to Christ Jesus on the peripheries of life and society."

36

SAINT BONAVENTURE
(c.1217 – 1274)
A leader in the Franciscan movement at a critical time

In the history of religious orders the charismatic founder sometimes begins a movement that is unsustainable in its original form. It then falls to a talented follower to organize the group and put structures in place. Such was the case with Bonaventure of Bagnoregio.

When studying for a Master's degree in Paris, Giovanni di Fidanza met followers of Saint Francis of Assisi. They so impressed him that he joined the Franciscans. He wrote: "The Church began with simple fishermen and was subsequently enriched by very distinguished and wise teachers; the religion of Blessed Francis was not established by the prudence of men but by Christ." He was clothed in the Franciscan habit about the year 1243 and took the name Bonaventure.

Bonaventure had been a talented student of theology at the University of Paris. Tensions were building between university masters and the new orders of friars, such as the Franciscans and Dominicans, who were beginning to occupy university chairs. The right of the friars to teach was challenged, and their style of religious life was questioned. They did not live in monasteries; they were in the streets spreading the Gospel. Bonaventure wrote a text, *Evangelical Perfection*, describing how the mendicant orders, and specifically the Franciscans, were following the Gospels in professing vows of poverty, chastity, and obedience. Bonaventure was officially recognized as a doctor and master at the University of Paris.

Minister General

In 1257 Bonaventure had to leave academic life when he was elected Minister General by a general chapter of the Franciscans. Bonaventure would serve the order for seventeen years.

By the time Bonaventure had been elected to leadership, the Franciscans had experienced a rapid expansion. Now no longer a small group walking the countryside preaching the Gospel, staying wherever they found shelter, and supported by the generosity of those whom they met, the order now numbered in the thousands, and it was Bonaventure's task to organize this movement.

Tensions arose within the group with different interpretations of the legacy of Saint Francis. Bonaventure collected material and remembrances from those who had known Francis. He wrote *Legend of Saint Francis*, a work identified by the Franciscan general chapter of 1263 as the official biography. The order needed structure and, following Saint Francis' determination, it needed to be faithful to the hierarchical Church. To maintain its structure and spirit, Bonaventure saw the need for a theological foundation.

Theologian

Bonaventure drew his theological insights from the lived experience of Saint Francis. Francis in his imitation of Christ made the Lord present for his time. In Bonaventure's theology God's very nature is love and this love, expressed within the Trinity, overflows into the created world. All creation bears the imprint of the Creator. All creation has the capacity to reflect the Creator as triune.

In 1259 Bonaventure wrote *The Soul's Journey into God*. He planned this work while at Mount La Verna where, thirty-three years before, Saint Francis had received the stigmata. Francis saw a vision of a winged seraph in the form of a crucifix. Meditating on the experience of Francis, Bonaventure understood the six wings of the Seraph to be six stages of the soul's journey leading to a final stage of union with God.

Influenced by the mystical theology of Pseudo-Dionysius, Bonaventure held that reason can reach a point where it no longer sees. But love can go beyond reason. Pope Benedict XVI, who as a young scholar studied Bonaventure, wrote "Saint Bonaventure was fascinated by this vision which converged with his own Franciscan spirituality. It is precisely in the dark night of the Cross that divine love appears in its full grandeur; where reason no longer sees, love sees" *(Great Christian Thinkers)*.

According to Bonaventure, the goal of the spiritual life is to be a contemplative, to be centered in God. Bonaventure taught that we come to know God by contemplating the humanity of Christ. He wrote, "There is no other path but through the burning love of the Crucified."

Bonaventure's emphasis on having an interior life, a life in relationship with God, is a timely message for today's world. Bonaventure scholar, Sr. Ilia Delio, O.S.F., writes: "The lack of interiority…is becoming increasingly apparent in our contemporary culture which is media saturated. …Only when God, the image in whom we are created, is the basis of the human spiritual quest, is the fullness of happiness and peace attained" *(Simply Bonaventure)*.

Canonized in 1482, Saint Bonaventure was declared a Doctor of the Church by Pope Sixtus V in 1588. His feast day is July 15.

37

ELIJAH, THE PROPHET

The Prophet Elijah was involved in two of the more dramatic events described in the First Book of Kings in the Old Testament. Both events took place on mountains, places on the earth considered closer to God. On Mount Carmel, Elijah defeated Baal, a pagan idol. On Mount Horeb, he renewed his relationship with the true God of Israel.

A Contest on Mount Carmel

The King and Queen of Israel, Ahab and Jezebel, were followers of Baal, the Canaanite god of storm and fertility. In opposition to Baal, the prophet Elijah declared a drought in Israel. "There shall be neither dew nor rain during these years, except by my word" *(1 Kgs 17:1)*. King Ahab assembled all Israel on Mount Carmel to witness a contest between Baal and the God of Israel. Elijah challenged the people: "How long will you straddle the issue? If the Lord is God, follow him; if Baal, follow him" *(1 Kgs 18:21)*.

Elijah instructed the worshipers of Baal to choose a young bull, cut it into two pieces and place one piece on a pile of wood. They were not to light a fire, but to call on their god, Baal, to ignite the wood. The prophets of Baal prayed, they hopped around the altar, but there was no response. Elijah taunted them: "Call louder, for he is a god and may be meditating, or may have retired, or may be on a journey" *(1 Kgs 18:27)*. The text concludes, "But there was not a sound; no one answered, and no one was listening" *(1 Kgs 18:29).*

Then Elijah prepared an altar on which he placed the other piece of the young bull. He ordered water to be poured on the holocaust and the wood. He then summoned the God of Abraham, Isaac, and Jacob to show the power of Israel's God. At this prayer, fire came down and destroyed the holocaust, the wood, and the altar. Nothing was left. Seeing this, the people proclaimed, "The Lord is God! The Lord is God!" *(1 Kgs 18:39)*

The Problem with Idols

An idol need not be a nature god like Baal. An idol can be a good we ask to be a god. For example, if I ask my job or some accomplishment to provide all the meaning and worth I deeply desire, I am asking too much. Only God can fulfill our deepest desires.

Idols never satisfy. Temporarily, idols produce satisfaction, but they are insubstantial food for the hungers of the heart. Possessions, titles, reputations, money, achievements all may be very appropriate in the life of an individual. But, our need is for a true center in our lives, for a source of worth and meaning that no trophy can provide.

Our true value comes from the Lord who loved us into life, and who accompanies us on our journey. Until we engage the transcendent Presence that haunts our lives, and live into that relationship, our lives are insubstantial. A small god results in a small person. I cannot grow past my god. And I am hurting whomever or whatever I am asking to be my god.

Elijah challenges us, "How long will you straddle the issue?"

Mount Horeb, the Mountain of God

After his great triumph, Elijah was still in trouble. Queen Jezebel was pursuing him. He became despondent, sat down in a deserted place, and prayed for death. But the Lord had further need of his services. Twice an angel came and ministered to Elijah, saying to him, "Get up and eat!" With revived spirits, Elijah traveled forty days and forty nights to Horeb, "God's mountain."

Elijah's journey to Horeb is reminiscent of Moses' journey in the desert to Sinai. It is thought the two mountains may actually be the same place. On Sinai, Moses made a covenant with the Lord. On Mount Horeb, Elijah renews his relationship with the Lord.

Elijah is invited to stand at the mouth of his cave, and the Lord will pass by. Standing outside the cave he experiences, first, a mighty destructive wind, and then an earthquake, and then a fire. The Lord was in none of these forces of nature. But then came "the sound of thin silence" *(1 Kgs 20:12)*. In this absence of sound, Elijah 'hears' the presence of God! The noise and distraction of idols has died down. Elijah is now a person available to the Lord. God has been waiting in the silence to have Elijah's attention. The prophet finds a reason to live!

Renewal occurs by returning to one's roots, and re-establishing a relationship with the Lord. Lent is a time for acknowledging idols, our false gods, and returning to the service of the true God. If we establish times of quiet for prayer and reflection we may also come to know ourselves better. The true God reveals to us our true selves.

Carmel and Elijah

The first Carmelites on Mount Carmel were well aware that they lived on a mountain associated with the prophet Elijah. They settled in a valley by the Spring of Elijah. In time Carmelites claimed a special relationship with the prophet, even at one time claiming he was their founder. Today Elijah serves as a special inspiration to Carmelites. He was the desert-dweller who challenged idols on behalf of the true God. Carmelites find in him both the contemplative and prophetic dimensions of their lives. The Carmelite Order has adopted the claim of the Prophet Elijah for its motto: "With zeal I have been zealous for the Lord God of Hosts" *(1 Kgs 19:14)*.

38

JOSEPH, THE DREAMER
A Man of Faith Followed His Dreams

Saint Joseph is introduced quickly in Matthew's Gospel, and he disappears by the time of Jesus' public ministry. His story is slender in details, but immensely meaningful for salvation history. Four brief dreams are the lynchpins for Joseph's story. In their starkness, the dreams mirror age-old archetypal stories of our human journey. A person goes forth in life, endures trials, wins the prize, and returns home with greater maturity.

First Dream

> "Joseph, son of David, do not be afraid to take Mary your wife into your home"
>
> *(Mt 1: 20)*

Joseph's story begins with a challenging but reassuring summons to go forth in life. Joseph wrestled with the prospect of taking on an enormous responsibility. Through it all he is silent; the Spirit is speaking. Joseph's famous silence (he speaks not one word in the Gospels!) indicates he is listening. Joseph is "a righteous man." He listens with faith.

Often, when people are moving into a more mature phase of their journey in life, something has interrupted their lives. It may be a profound religious insight, it may be a serious setback, or a deeply felt loss. The person moves in an uncharted direction toward a different identity. The Bible only hints at Joseph's travails. The journey to Bethlehem and a birth in a manger let the reader know that Joseph had to struggle with life's contingencies. St. Luke tells us "there was no room for them in the inn."

Second Dream

"Rise, take the child and his mother, flee to Egypt..."
(Mt 2:13)

Herod is looking for Jesus. Joseph stays with his commitment and finds himself challenged to protect his family. The Holy Family is in danger. He and his family flee to a foreign land, a place without familiar supports.

When such a phase in life has been told in countless stories, archetypal images express the experience. It is like battling dragons, entering a dark forbidding forest, being swallowed by a whale. It is a precarious phase in life, with danger at the edges. The stories say, stay in the dark, remain in Egypt, learn what needs to be learned; Herod still lives!

Maturity in life usually comes through trials. Those who have had to wrestle with a problem, or problems, often emerge with a deeper, more mature personality. The wounds and scars of life have given shape to a resilient, more self-confident person. From a faith perspective, the individual becomes less ego-centered and more God-centered. This individual story is part of a larger story God is telling.

Third and Fourth Dreams

"Rise, take the child and his mother, and go to the land of Israel..."
(Mt 2: 20)

Herod has died. Patience, trust, and continual deep listening move Joseph to a new situation. The danger subsides, the journey is renewed, and eventually his pilgrimage takes him back home. At first he was going to return to Judea, but once again, "because he had been warned in a dream" *(Mt 2: 22)* he made his home in Nazareth, a town in Galilee. Joseph begins a family life, works in a trade, and becomes a well-known citizen in town.

In parallel mythic stories, when dark forces are engaged, eventually the dragon is defeated, the center of the forest is reached, and the pearl, the treasure, or the chalice is recovered. The hero returns home with the prize. G.K. Chesterton wrote, "The purpose of all journey is to come home."

Our Dreams

Unexpected guidance can come from dreams, intuitions, serendipitous occurrences. The Magi followed a star to arrive in Bethlehem, and they followed a dream to return home "by another way" *(Mt 2:12)*. Because it is a graced world with the presence of God accompanying and sustaining it, all of creation is sacramental. Any part of it, including our dreams, may speak to us of the nearness of God's Spirit, the presence of the Reign of God. St. Teresa of Avila said, "I believe that in each little thing created by God, there is more than what is understood, even if it is a little ant" *(Interior Castle, IV, 2, 2)*.

It is not necessarily that God is speaking directly to us in our dreams. It is what we do with these unexpected events. It is our relationship to the events that may offer guidance. Those occasions that shimmer with mystery, such as dreams or nature's marvels, may evoke a readiness in us to be led into a deeper life, a more fulfilling life, a life more closely related to the story God is telling.

In a morning meditation on a past feast of Saint Joseph, Pope Francis asked the Saint to grant all of us "the ability to dream because when we dream great things, good things, we draw near to God's dream, what God dreams about us" *(L'Osservatore Romano)*.

Carmel, a Place of Dreams

In 2020 the two Generals of the OCARM and OCD branches of the Carmelite family wrote a letter on the occasion of the 150th anniversary of the proclamation of St. Joseph as Patron of the Universal Church. Addressed to the Carmelite family, the Generals wrote:

> The Word came to Joseph in a dream, which we may understand as his prayer, his interiority. We might say that every Carmel is a place of dreams: prayer is like a dream, that has within it

a secret message. A Carmelite community is a group of people that dreams of making of its own home a new Jerusalem, people who share the dream of the prophet for a better world, people who allow themselves to be captured every day by the dream of salvation... .

Saint Joseph protects Carmel, not only because he protects it from hostile attack and from every adversity, but also because he helps Carmel to remain firm in the simplicity and profundity of its identity. With his being just he points the way that we must follow and the goal for which we must strive. In this sense, there is no doubt that our veneration of Saint Joseph is not only a devotion or pious practice, but rather a life plan, that is an integral part of the charismatic heritage of Carmel. Together with Mary, Joseph is the Gospel icon in which we Carmelites may see and understand what it means to live "in allegiance to Jesus Christ." It is right then that we continue to turn to him as our father and patron, but also as a faithful friend and reliable guide in our following in the footsteps of Jesus."

39

A MINOR ORDER
The Carmelites

I joined the Carmelites because I liked the men who taught me at Joliet Catholic High School. For all I knew, the Order started in a basement in Chicago. I learned more later, but it was too late.

The Order actually started on a mountainous ridge, Mount Carmel, near the port of Haifa in Israel. On this mountain, in Old Testament times, the prophet Elijah defeated the priests of Baal. In the early 1200's c.e. a group of men took up residence in a valley on Mount Carmel to live a prayerful life of silence and solitude. They lived on the land of Jesus, their liege Lord. Their chapel was dedicated to Mary. These men elected their leadership, and asked the Patriarch of Jerusalem to give them a Rule.

Carmelites lived less than 100 years on Mount Carmel, and then abandoned the mountain because of constant tensions between the Christians and the Saracens. They migrated to Europe where, in the words of one historian, they continued the tradition of founding communities "in rapidly declining neighborhoods." They joined the Augustinians, Dominicans, and Franciscans, the mendicant Orders of the Middle Ages, in serving the newly emerging urban centers.

These facts we would learn in the novitiate. Along with studying the Carmelite tradition, we spent time in chapel. Four windows in the chapel had sayings of Carmelite Saints, in Latin. Translated, they were in order:

> Either to suffer or to die
> Not to die, just suffer
> Suffer and be despised
> Suffer and be quiet
> But, the food was good.

The novitiate at that time was located on a farm, and we did farm chores. Most of us were from cities, and some adjustments had to be made. Men were fainting when the pigs were slaughtered. And we learned further sayings of the Carmelites such as, In the evening of life we will be judged by our love *(St. John of the Cross)*, and, Our God is nothing but mercy and love *(St. Thérèse of Lisieux)*. Half the class made it to the end of the novitiate, and professed vows.

Carmelites serve the needs of the Church, whatever they may be. But, always, the intent is to live in allegiance to Jesus Christ, with a listening heart. The Order is divided into smaller units called Provinces. Our particular Province serves the Church in six countries, with men on independent assignment in Rome. Usually we live in community working in schools, parishes, retreat centers, and shrines. The Province has had a longstanding tradition of serving the church in higher education.

With an 800-year history, a religious community cannot be too arrogant. We have had certain centuries when few things went right; other centuries were better. The long view helps get past the crises of the day.

One of the men from our Province spent a lifetime studying the Order and wrote four volumes on our history. Last year he finished a one-volume digest of this work, shortly before dying at age 95. At the end of this historical study, he observed that the Carmelites have never been a very important Order in the Church. "Friars minor" suits us better than the Franciscans. Through the centuries the Order has shared the life of the Church, sometimes making a humble but distinctive contribution. He hopes we could say, at least, "without Carmel the story of the Church would not be quite the same."

40

MEMORIES
of
The Seminary, Civil Rights, and a 'Contemplative Prophet'

Because of the mob storming the Capitol Building January 6, 2021 and the events around it, I have been remembering my time in Washington, D.C. I lived there 1961 to 1965 studying theology at Whitefriars Hall, the Carmelite school of theology. Vatican II was in session. During that time I made solemn vows in the Carmelite Order, and was ordained a priest.

It was the time of the Civil Rights Movement. As seminarians we became involved in the protests. I have always considered our activities in the civil rights movement to be a significant part of our formation, our training in Carmelite life.

Our religious superior in those days was Fr. Peter Hinde. He had been a fighter pilot in WWII stationed on Okinawa. After the war Peter joined the Carmelites whom he knew from attending Mount Carmel High School in Chicago. After ordination, and a few years teaching in high school, Peter volunteered to live in the Order's desert house in Wolfnitz, Austria.

Wolfnitz was the site of a hermit community echoing the original Carmelite community on Mount Carmel in Palestine. Silence and solitude provided an environment for contemplative prayer. Peter lived that eremitical life for three years. He then volunteered for our missions in Latin America.

However, superiors thought he should be the director of the students studying theology in Washington. He would bring a contemplative spirit to the theology house. But, contemplation is the deepest source of compassion for a world in need of social justice. Fr. Peter's prayer convinced him that the civil rights movement was the great social justice activity of our time.

Civil Rights Movement

Fr. Peter allowed and encouraged the students to participate in demonstrations and protests on behalf of justice. We joined the March on Washington in August, 1963 and were on the Mall in front of the Lincoln Memorial when Dr. Martin Luther King gave his "I Have a Dream" speech.

Our classes required reading many theological texts. But a document that has remained in my memory is Dr. King's Letter from a Birmingham Jail written in April, 1963. Leading a protest against segregation in Birmingham, Alabama, Dr. King was arrested for not having a parade permit.

From the jail Dr. King wrote a long letter recounting the evils of segregation. In particular he expressed disappointment in the white "moderate" including the white church and its leadership which voiced support for civil rights, but criticized protests. In truth, we saw few Catholic leaders in the early days of the movement.

While Congress was debating the Civil Rights Act of 1964, our Whitefriars Hall community participated with seminarians of all faiths in 24 hour vigils in front of the Lincoln Memorial. After sixty days of debate in Congress the law was passed. It banned segregation in public accommodations and prohibited discrimination on the basis of race, color, religion, sex, or national origin. This law also prohibited discrimination on the basis of sex, as well as race, in hiring, promoting, and firing.

The next year, in August, 1965, Congress passed the Voting Rights Act. This Act banned literacy tests and other barriers to voting. It said the government could send federal registrars and observers to register new voters and oversee elections. It also required pre-clearance of new election-related legislations in places (mainly states) with a history of voting rights discrimination.

It does the soul good remembering these documents and the moral issues they address. The fundamental issue of human rights is still with us today.

Remembering Peter Hinde, O. Carm.

I continue to remember Fr. Peter Hinde, the religious superior who taught us the connection between prayer and social justice. After five years in charge of theology students, he was granted permission to serve in our Carmelite missions. Fr. Peter ministered among communities of the poor in Latin America. He was acquainted with those martyred in El Salvador: the four Catholic women missionaries from the United States, the six Jesuits with their housekeeper and her daughter in San Salvador, and Archbishop Oscar Romero (canonized by Pope Francis in 2018), assassinated by the military while saying Mass. Peter co-founded Christians for Peace in El Salvador (CRISPAZ) whose goal was to educate North Americans about the reasons for the suffering of the people of Latin America.

With the idea of "reverse mission," Peter and Mercy Sister Betty Campbell, a nurse and co-worker, opened Tabor House in Washington, D.C., a community hosting missionaries and exiles from Latin America. The community moved to San Antonio, Texas, and eventually to Ciudad Juarez, Mexico, across the border from El Paso, Texas.

For the past 25 years, Tabor House has been in Ciudad Juarez accompanying exploited factory workers, abused women, and refugees from Central America. Tabor House welcomed delegations of US citizens from universities, parishes and seminaries who came to the border for week-long immersion experiences.

This past year of the pandemic, 2020, Peter became ill from Covid-19. After time in a hospice in El Paso, Peter died from complications due to the virus. He was 97 years old. A few days before he died, Peter and Sister Betty received a CRISPAZ peace award for three decades of service to El Salvador.

Carmelite Provincial Fr. Carl Markelz said, "Peter had two pillars in his life: activism and prayer. He was a true contemplative prophet. He brings to mind Pope Francis' statement – that 'the pastor has to smell like the sheep.' That was Peter."

May Peter Hinde, O. Carm., rest in peace, and may the arc of history continue to bend toward justice in the Americas.

AFTERWORD

The title of this work, *Immersed in Mystery*, is a phrase used by a friend and psychologist Gerald May who was attempting to assess what was good and and what was bad in his life. He found it difficult to make a final assessment of either. A bad situation may have provided a context for a number of good experiences. Similarly, a good situation may have had to give way to unwanted difficulties. Unable to make a final assessment he concluded we are immersed in mystery.

Telling Our Story

The brief articles in this work are based on the conviction that God loves each of us specifically, uniquely, eternally, and that life is a process of divinization with our deepest desires motivated, invited, and clarified by God's desire for us. We move and mature in a world of grace. Our desires becoming more and more consonant with God's desire.

Apparently, we need to tell stories. Stories help us make sense of our lives. We need to tell our story so we can enter it more fully and own it. A Carmelite telling of our journey says we wake up in the middle of a love story. Someone has wounded our heart with love and made it ache for fulfillment. Our journey in life is a search for that presence, now seemingly absent.

Our experiences along the way are never only human or only divine. They are always both, a world permeated with grace. To be human is be God-touched and God-targeted. Our pilgrimage through life is a realization, an awakening, to the abiding Presence of one who is "always already there." The basic pattern in many of the articles in this work is the paschal mystery, the dying and rising of Christ. In order for there to be change, transformation, new life, something must be let go, surrendered.

When God Tells Our Story

Ultimately we cannot assess our lives from within our lives. The former archbishop of Canterbury, Rowan Williams, made this observation: "A human life is given its unity and its intelligibility from outside; when God pulls taut the slack thread of desire, bonding it to himself, the muddled and painful litter of experience is gathered together and given direction." The final assessment is stated clearly by Saint John of the Cross: 'In the evening you will be examined in love."

Our human story is a small but very meaningful part of a much larger story, the story of God's creation. Pope Francis in his encyclical on the environment, *Laudato Si*, offers this breath-taking vision: "The ultimate destiny of the universe is in the fullness of God, which has already been obtained by the risen Christ, the measure of the maturity of all things" (#83).

Recommended Carmelite Websites

FOR MORE INFORMATION ABOUT THE CARMELITES TODAY,
OUR SPIRITUALITY AND OUR MINISTRIES WORLDWIDE, VISIT:

The Carmelite Order
ocarm.org

The Most Pure Heart of Mary Province
carmelites.net

Center for Carmelite Studies at Catholic University of America
carmelites.info/CenterForCarmeliteStudies

Carmelite Institute of North America
carmeliteinstitute.net

Instituto de las Americas
institutocarmelitano.carmelitas.org

FOR A LISTING OF CARMELITE PROVINCES WORLDWIDE, VISIT:
carmelites.info/provinces

FOR A LISTING OF MONASTERIES OF CARMELITE NUNS, VISIT:
carmelites.info/nuns

FOR A LISTING OF CARMELITE HERMITAGES, PLEASE VISIT:
carmelites.info/hermits

FOR A LISTING OF SITES ABOUT LAY CARMELITES:
carmelites.info/lay carmel

FOR A LISTING OF AFFILIATED CONGREGATIONS AND INSTITUTES:
carmelites.info/congregations

FOR OUR WORK WITH THE UNITED NATIONS, VISIT:
carmelitengo.org

FOR MORE INFORMATION ABOUT PUBLICATIONS, VISIT:
carmelites.info/publications